The Dynamic Studio

Copyright ©2012 by **Philip Johnston**

ISBN 978-0-9581905-5-8   Version 1.0

The Dynamic Studio | InsideMusicTeaching.com

Also by Philip Johnston

Not Until You've Done Your Practice (1989)

The Practice Revolution (2002)

The PracticeSpot Guide to Promoting your Teaching Studio (2003)

Practiceopedia: (2007)

Scales Bootcamp: (2009)

For more help and online resources

www.insidemusicteaching.com

www.thedynamicstudio.com

Contents

Our ideas, like orange-plants, spread out in proportion to the size of the box which imprisons the roots.

Edward Bulwer Lytton

The case for a Dynamic Studio

Why we can't use yesterday's lessons
to teach today's students

The case for a Dynamic Studio

As I'm writing this, it's the second decade of the 21st Century; things haven't turned out quite as Stanley Kubrik might have imagined, but anybody teleported here from 1950 should still be nicely bewildered.

Just about anybody, that is.

If a music student from 1950 were to teleport into a music studio of this decade, they'd feel oddly at home. Various technological curiosities notwithstanding, the structure, content, pacing and expectations of the lessons themselves really wouldn't be so different from what they would have been used to:

The student is *given pieces to practice*;
The student goes home and *practices* those pieces.
The student *comes to their next lesson*;
The teacher *hears the pieces*;
The teacher *issues corrections and recommendations*;
The student goes home and *practices again*.
Lather, rinse and repeat until it's time for a new piece.
Oddly at home.

As 21st Century music teachers, we could all—with a little attention to what we wear, colloquialism coaching and cellphone withdrawal therapy—be substitute studio music teachers in the 1950s; we'd fit in just fine.

I intend no disrespect when I say this. Music teaching has good reasons when it proudly talks about tradition, and ours has not been a profession of frivolous change, or reform simply because it's been a while since the last one. There's also plenty of evidence that the process *works*—the world is filled with symphony orchestras and jazz ensembles and bands and college music programs made up of people who learned to play Very Well Thank You with lessons just like these.

But here's the thing. All these musicians only got that far because they *stayed* in their lessons. More than ever before, for reasons we'll look at throughout this book, today's students are not.

We can hardly blame them. These are students used to going from knowing nothing about a subject to being able to write a detailed school paper using two mouse clicks and a single search term. These are students who have played computer games that allow them to become professional golfers, or tennis players—or even musicians—and who are then winning virtual contests and dazzling virtual crowds within minutes of picking up their virtual racquet or guitar for the first time; and who then, having been gifted evidence that they've already *excelled* (virtually, but without virtue), will be actively looking for a different game.

These are students who are maintaining half a dozen different texted conversations on their phone, while YouTube, two different homework assignments and Facebook are open in different windows on the laptop in front of them, as their music player is randomly cycling between tens of thousands of songs on a playlist that is almost certainly not the same as anyone else's in the world.

These are students who are bombarded with stories of overnight successes—of reality-tv talent show auditions, high school basketball drafts and twenty-something tech billion-aires—in a world where 15 minutes of fame is anyone's for the taking, but probably 10 minutes longer than anybody would want to be stuck with the same career.

These are kids raised by the first generation of parents in history who were themselves told as kids that they could Do

Anything and Be Anything, and who now unsurprisingly expect their own kids to Do and Be *Everything*; kids whose minds move with the speed of CGI-infused smash-cut music videos, Amazon 1-click buying and games-console decision making.

These are students who take part in more activities before and after school than ever before, coupled with an ephemeral attention span and voracious appetite for "show me something new" that prefers buffets to committing to any dish in particular, because they know the true cost of doing something is not measured in dollars, but in the infinitely fractalling list of other things they *could have been doing with that time*, but are now *missing out on*.

In fact, that above all else. These are students wary of commitment, of the maddeningly incalculable loss that opportunity cost represents; the sheer *instant everythingness* of the internet giving the illusion that all these things—skydiving and dentistry and playing the cello and dancing and making a million dollars and helping babies in Africa and going to Mars and being a jockey and inventing new types of breakfast cereal and repairing cars and designing computer games and being the President and never being the President—that all these things are possible in one lifetime. Like never before, these are students who can see *all* of life's possibilities, rendered vivid and searchable, as though they're commodities on a shelf. To spent time with any one of these things is to steal time from everything else; to *commit* is to *miss out...*

...hardly surprising then that these are also students for whom traditional music lessons are too structured, too gradual, too *slow* to be a long-term option.

Which is exactly why—traditional or not, successful in the past or not—we cannot continue to teach the same way we were taught, because the students we're working with are *not* simply more contemporary versions of what we once were.

They're just not.

In most of the ways that count for anything, they're not actually from the same planet.

This disjuncture between *what our training has prepared us for* and *who we are actually working with* has very real consequences for music teachers individually, and the profession as a whole. It means high turnover rates, gaps in our schedules where students used to be, and the constant fear that any student we teach—*any* student—could be about to call to "take a break". Teaching is still fulfilling, but increasingly, it's also fraught.

Music teachers have two choices at this point. They can simply accept that higher attrition is a fact of life in the modern teaching world, and pump ever increasing resources into advertising to keep the leaking bucket full.

Or they can rethink just what it is that their studio *does*, so that it's not only able to *attract* today's students, but *retain* them.

That does, of course, mean looking at things in a completely different way.

Turning an *immovable object* into an *irresistible force*

It's only when you really read through a typical studio policy carefully that it becomes clear just how emphatically *well-defined* traditional music lessons are. Lessons are *this long*, and on *these days*. The *practice expectations* are as follows. *Studio recitals* are held in these months. *All students are expected* to prepare for *these competitions*. The *beginner book we use* can be ordered from *this* store.

With all these prescriptions and proscriptions, studio policies have become more than just guidelines; somewhere, when we weren't looking, they have evolved into *templates*, locking teachers, parents and students into The Way We Do Things.

Again, there are good reasons for this conservatism. As experienced teachers, we have seen for ourselves what works and what doesn't, and to make our finest teaching moments *reproducible*, we mandate the conditions that led to those outcomes. We understand well what we offer, and how we offer it; we know what resources will get the job done; we're clear on the expectations we have of our students, and of the parents who support their lessons.

> **"...traditional music lessons are, too structured, too gradual, too *slow* to be a long term option."**

Our continued excellence is therefore founded not just on our commitment to but the *replication* of established standards and workflows.

But the inevitable consequence of replication is to create a studio that is essentially *static*: built upon pillars that are well crafted and thoughtfully placed, but immobile nonetheless.

This air of permanence makes sense when the aim is to preserve the best of what has gone before; it's why so many studio policies are almost word-for-word identical to what they had been a decade earlier. But preserving what has gone before doesn't make sense when the old approach is not working with new students.

This book proposes a different way forwards; a switch from *static*, tradition-based here's-how-we-do-things teaching to a *dynamic* studio, where *planning and precedence* takes a back seat to *opportunity and improvisation*. A studio in which if someone were to ask you "what will you be offering your students in a year from now", you can honestly—and proudly—say "I have no idea". A studio where your own skillset is constantly expanding, so that you can always be offering *more* and *different* and *new*. Where two dozen students can go through your studio and have two dozen *completely* different experiences. Where today is rarely exactly like yesterday, and statements like "all students should" and "my expectations are" are replaced with "What if...?" and "Why wouldn't we...?".

It's about switching the focus from curriculum and methods to being able to *engage* today's students compellingly enough to *keep* them.

And these are students worth keeping. They might be impatient, and relentlessly multitasking and Googlefied and ambitious and distractible, but they're also—with daylight second—the most exciting generation of students that teachers of any type have ever seen.

How this book works

THIS BOOK IS NOT A HOW-TO guide, or a method. You'll find no information in here on how to teach, save for the warning that you should be wary of books that tell you how to teach.

Instead, it's simply designed to start a conversation, by challenging music teachers to ask themselves a confronting, but ultimately liberating question:

Given the extraordinary changes music teaching finds itself surrounded by, if you had the opportunity to hit "reset" on how your studio currently operates and build it again from scratch, what might your new job look like?

What time-honoured elements of music teaching would you *retain*, or perhaps *rethink*, or *dial up*, or *dial down* or *discontinue entirely?* Which skills would you be seeking to develop with your students, and which might you abandon as being no longer relevant? How might that new studio be *equipped* or *purged* to achieve those ends? What might a *schedule* look like? What would *practicing* look like? What would practicing be *for?* As students currently know it, would practice even *exist?* How would you parcel up *time* within the lesson? What new *incentives* or *goals* might you have in place to get students excited about the future? How would you give students critical *feedback*, and a *sense of their own progress?* What lessons can be learned from the non-musical leisure time activities that *do* already capture their imaginations and attention?

> "You're not a slave to tradition, or to a studio policy, or to What Other Teachers Do... you're free to create whatever you can imagine."

And how can you possibly make the whole experience of spending time in your studio *engaging* and *addictive* enough to compete with the Great Endlessly Varied Everything Else that your students could be doing instead?

This book will provide suggested answers to the original hypothetical, but it does so by way of themes and examples, rather than directives. The tone is informal, not scholarly (none of my books are remotely scholarly); instead it's designed to feel as if you and I were discussing this over coffee—as though you had just posed that studio tear-down hypothetical to me.

We'd need more than one cup to finish that conversation, is all—this is fertile territory for a discussion: it's essentially asking *if your studio could be anything at all, what would it be?*; a question that's as exciting as it is divisive, and worthy of a book-length response.

Your own answers to the core hypothetical might not match mine at all. That's fine. Think of the whole thing as being like browsing a magazine of *Great Ideas For Your New Kitchen* ahead of a renovation; you're not compelled to adopt any of the magazine's ideas, but you will come away a lot more excited and better informed about *types* of changes that are possible...and suddenly much more aware of the limitations of the old kitchen you've been working with this whole time.

What's exciting about all this...

...is that the hypothetical at the core of this book *is not actually hypothetical at all*. You *do* have the opportunity to tear down the way your studio operates and build it again from scratch. It's your studio; you decide what happens.

Let me say that again, because for most music teachers—frustrated by how things are, aching with a sense that there *has* to be more to their professional life than *this*—it's a realisation that's yet to truly dawn:

It's *your* studio. *You* decide what happens. You're not a slave to tradition, or a studio policy, or What Other Teachers Do, or What You've Been Doing For The Past Decade or What Students Think Lessons Are For At The Moment; you're free to create whatever you can imagine.

We'll look in depth at *processes* that facilitate change, and the types of *thinking* that informs those choices, but right now the easiest way to get a sense of how this all works is to dive straight in, and look at an example:

The Dynamic Studio at work: the 10 minute theory conundrum

The suggestions outlined throughout this book deliberately target everyday, concrete teaching realities, rather than lofty, abstract pedagogical constructs. I wanted to build all of this around issues that music teachers regularly have to confront, so that any changes are targeting the very things we actually spend most of our time *doing*, rather than those things that pedagogues spend time *theorising about*.

So let's start by simply imagining a studio that has always started each lesson with 10 minutes of theory. Not so hard to imagine; there are countless music lessons taking place right now that *did* start that way.

Let's also imagine it's become increasingly obvious that students are finding those theory sessions tedious. (With all due respect to music theory, that's also not so hard to imagine.)

The fact that an emergent problem like this demands a *response* of some kind is not at issue: both Static and Dynamic studios will try to make the bad situation better. Static Studios are not blind to problems, nor are they indifferent to the concerns of their students, nor are they unambitious on their behalf.

The telling difference—and the reason that a switch to a Dynamic approach is so important for working with today's students—is in the *range* of options available to both. The Static Studio is bound by tradition. The Dynamic Studio is free to try any solution it can imagine.

So in our example, the Static Studio will almost certainly have its hands tied somewhat by its own studio policy or pro- spectus which (inconveniently now) talks about a "compulsory theory component" and stresses that "all students are expected to prepare for theory examinations". It also has to deal with the reality that the studio itself has a decade of history where every lesson has started with 10 minutes of theory.

Those are the constraints; any changes made by the Static Studio need to accommodate that framework. So the teacher might decide to (1) be *more animated* while they're explaining all those time signatures and leading notes or (2) *switch* to a *more engaging text* or (3) *send a note home* reminding students and parents of the importance of music theory, much as fibre is important in a good diet.

But this is tinkering, not change; the solutions under consideration here do nothing to fundamentally alter the status quo—*which is precisely why they're the solutions under consideration.* The result will simply be more of the same, albeit perhaps with a different book, some added enthusiasm, and a list of reasons that Theory Matters. The theory segment itself will quickly return to being a drag, and fully one-third(!) of the weekly teaching time will continue to leave both teacher and students feeling flat.

> "...if you had the opportunity to tear down the way your studio currently operates and build it again from scratch, what might your new job look like?"

The absence of real change for a problem that affects a significant slice of every lesson like this will—be certain of this—cost that studio students. *Especially* today's students. The Static Studio might be bound by tradition, but the student is not bound to stay enrolled.

The question at the heart of this book is a simple one: *what would the same studio do if it knew it could do anything it liked?*

It's important to understand that the Dynamic Studio in our example is assumed to be no better at teaching theory, and has students who are finding the existing theory situation just as dull. But the Dynamic Studio has one huge advantage: it's not bound by any of conventions or self-imposed rules. This opens up possibilities that the Static Studio would never dare consider.

So...students are dreading theory? Let's start with (1) *Don't teach it any more.* Seriously. The world is *not* going to end, no matter what you may have been told as a student. Or (2) keep teaching it, but *rewrap it* as something engagingly practical in the context of a Learn To Improvise class. Or (3) handle it with *theory workshops* that meets fortnightly...in a park...with the lessons conducted while the group *walks.* Or (4) establish a *Theory And Pizza evening* on the first Tuesday of every month. Or (5) teach it *via Skype.* Or (6) find *software* so students can drill it at home. Or (7) *write your own theory book* that actually *is* engaging, and tailored for your students, with the content you wish other theory books would have. Or (8) *combine* with the other music teachers in your city to work on that book and *write a chapter each.* Or (9) have your *senior students* do some of the heavy lifting by *tutoring* beginners in theory. Or (10) introduce a competitive element and train up a *studio Theory Team* to go head-to-head with another studio in an interstudio Theory Olympics. Or (11) start *assembling YouTube playlists* of the best theory explanations you've found online, so students can effectively cover it themselves. Or (12) make such videos yourself. Or (13) announce that theory *only* happens in March, August and November, but as *intensive blitz-type programs,* giving you the same depth of coverage in the course of a year, but also giving you 9 months of theory-free zones. Or (14) *seamlessly integrate it* with your student's instrumental studies, so there are no sheets to fill in, just conversations about each piece. Or (15) create incentives with a *martial-arts style belt system* for your theory offerings, so students can progress from white to yellow to green to blue to brown to black. Or (16) partner with another studio so that *you teach theory to their students*, and *they to yours*, to keep it separate and fresh. Or (17) have every month *sponsored* by a different theory topic— March is about Key Signatures, April is about Intervals, May is about Cadences—much the same way that *Sesame Street* used to have episodes sponsored by letters of the alphabet. Or (18) use a big theory *Spin Wheel*, which any student with a birthday gets to spin to *set the topic*—or even whether there *is* any theory being taught at the moment or not— which lasts until the next birthday

> "There are no constraints. It's your studio. You decide what happens."

spin. Or (19) set up a theory *geocache*, where you hide questions for students to uncover. Or (20) have radio-style theory quizzes, which you turn into podcasts. Or (21) slash *10* minutes to *5*, but go *fast*, with a countdown timer pushing both teacher and student through the *same content* in *half the time*. Or (22) make the 10 minutes of theory an *elective*, for those who actively choose a theory supplement to their lessons...

...there are no constraints.
It's your studio.
You decide what happens.

You might as well decide something that makes your job an engaging, endlessly surprising, creative, energising and *fun* way to spend tens of thousands of hours of your one and only life...

...because over the course of most music teacher's careers, that's the sort of time we're talking about.

When *options* actually become your *future*

There are 22 potential solutions on the example list above—hardly scratching the surface of possible responses to this one problem alone—but it's important to understand that all these options are not just bullet points on a page. They're *tickets* to *different possible futures*. They're different makes and models of how you could be spending your time from now on, which means that choosing between them is—not in the overblown sense of the expression, but quite literally—life-changing. The way you spend your hours and minutes in the future will be determined by the creative thinking you did today; it's worth considering such possibilities as carefully as the purchase of a new house, or a move interstate.

So let's take a moment and think through what just *one* of these options might actually mean, were you to adopt it. Let's shuffle those 21 cards, and choose...let's see...it's a 4...

...which means your studio *stops* offering theory as part of *regular lessons*, and instead introduces a *Theory And Pizza Evening* on the first Tuesday of every month.

What's important to understand here is if you were to adopt this, the teaching year that follows is now going to be *completely* different than it would have been otherwise...and completely different from the teaching years that any of the (still unselected) 21 options would have produced. Picture it for yourself, think through the ripples from this cast stone:

What will those Tuesday gatherings be like? Which of your students might be *laughing* for the first time in a theory lesson, instead of *looking at their watch?* How different will presenting key signatures feel when you're talking to 25 students at once, rather than presenting the same information to individual students on 25 separate occasions? What new studio resources might you want to get to make those presentations compelling? How much better will you get to know some of your students—and will they get to know *each other*—in a relaxed environment like that? What opportunities might then open up for you to engineer further studio initiatives based on these people working together?

> "...all these options are not just bullet points on a page. They're *tickets* to different possible *futures*.
>
> How do you want to be spending your time?"

What will the 25 sets of waiting parents talk to each other about as they come up the driveway to pick up their kids? What will they think when they hear a chorus of cheers coming from inside, and then see their child at a whiteboard taking a bow?

And when the Tuesday night has been and gone, *just how will you spend all those 10 minutes in every single lesson that you've now got back?*

Remember, all you started with was "The students are not enjoying the mandatory theory component". You could have decided just to suck it up—or worse still, expected your students to simply suck it up.

Or you could take a decision as CEO of your teaching studio—which is exactly what you are—and create *change*.

What's next:

Obviously this is very much a book about change, but we're not going to start with dramatic initiatives, Glorious 5 Year Plans or wrecking-ball rebuilds. Instead, the next chapter looks at ways to shake your existing studio; partly to see what falls out, but mostly so your students are suddenly aware of *movement*.

Shaking up the Static Studio

Tremors before the quake

Shaking up the Static Studio

As any marriage guidance counsellor will tell you, when comfortably-familiar is left on autopilot, you end up with *monotony*, a relationship-wrecker that seeds doom not through the presence of the bad, but the absence of the good.

This principle should be a cautionary tale to any Dynamic Studio because music teaching is founded on—and founders upon—the health of the relationship between teacher and student. If students are being delighted, challenged and surprised, then they'll find the lessons delightful, challenging and surprising. These are students with *reasons to stay*.

This is *not* the same thing as students who seem to have *no reason to leave*. In the case of the latter, even if the lessons are ticking all the right pedagogical boxes, once students are starting to have trouble telling one lesson from the next, and find themselves experiencing the same rewards, expectations, pacing, choice of language, workflow, resources and goals, then there's trouble looming. There's a fine line between consistency and torpor.

Managing that fine line has always been important in music teaching, but never more so than now. The world of our students is not one that tolerates anything that even remotely smacks of boredom. They'll click another link, change the song, load up a different game.

Switch to a different after-school activity.

What's so insidious about this is that when mere *same-old* is the problem, there won't necessarily be anything outstandingly awful that will flag itself to the teacher as being a potential lesson-killer. For the Static Studio, everything will seem to be running *just fine*, as it always has. Which means that when students leave, it can often come as a shock: "Lessons were going so well" is the lament "How could I fix something that wasn't broken?"

The problem here is that this post-departure analysis invokes the wrong cliché. Instead of *if it ain't broke*, the teacher should be thinking rolling stones and moss, familiarity and contempt, still waters running *tedious*.

Why the *rhythm* of lessons is worth disrupting

After just a few sessions with their teacher, students in any studio—Static or Dynamic—will start to become familiar with the rituals and priorities, patterns and challenges that power their lessons. Within that, there are inevitably recurring elements, architectures and values that create a sense of regularity, which in turn gives those lessons a heartbeat; a *rhythm*.

The rhythm is what gives students the sense that each week they can reasonably expect to have *this many* pieces to work on at once, *this type* of technical work to drill and *these sorts* of theory sheets to complete; that lessons themselves normally unfold in the *following manner,* and that their teacher expects them to get *these things* right above all else, and will usually write on their score for *these reasons* and mark the corrections in the *following way*; that students in this studio work towards *these targets*, using the *following resources,* and with *this amount of daily practice required.*

> "...when students leave, it can often come as a shock: "Lessons were going so well" is the lament "How could I fix something that wasn't broken?""

There's nothing wrong with students having expectations like these, or a studio having elements consistent enough for students to be able to form such expectations in the first place. In fact, the specifics that make up such expectations are what makes your studio *your* studio, and not somebody else's; a studio's rhythm is as unique as a fingerprint.

But if the student's assumptions are borne out too frequently, then the seeds are being sown for an eventual failure to engage, particularly for a generation that is used to *alternatives* and *upgrades* and *what's new*. In a world of change, stasis doesn't look like consistency; it looks like *dull*.

> "These are students with *reasons to stay.* This is *not* the same thing as students who seem to have *no reason to leave.*

Changing the rhythm of lessons is not about abandoning patterns in teaching, but it is about periodically confounding the expectations that such patterns create. It's about leaving students just a little off balance, making it harder for them to settle into any sense of "same old", because there *is* no same old.

Finding the right mix is a challenge; obviously you don't want your lessons to feel like they've been planned by a committee of manic-depressives with ADHD who have been randomly spiking each other's sandwiches with either Ritalin or marijuana, but nor can you afford for status quo to become the *only* quo. So how do you mix up your lessons without messing up your students?

This chapter looks at **9 structural elements of teaching** that are particularly prone to establishing patterns, and then at ways to disrupt those rhythms so that your studio always feels fresh...while still keeping intact the values and architecture that makes your studio *your* studio. Hence "shaking up", rather than "knocking down"; the primary aim is for your students to suddenly be aware of *motion*.

(1): Shaking up the order of attack

With normally only half an hour available for each lesson, most studios quickly learn that the most efficient way to get through everything is to have a sequence of events that acts as a virtual run-sheet. So lessons typically start with X, move on to Y, and conclude with Z.

The advantage to this approach is that with the order of attack being similar each time, there's then no need to have to re-lay groundwork for the various lesson elements the second time around. So while in the very first lesson, you might need to introduce the idea that all lessons start with X, in lessons thereafter, you can just get on with actually *starting* with X, rather than having to shovel the path clear first.

Likewise, 10 minutes into X, students will be anticipating Y, which makes Y a zero-preparation transition as well. And so on.

From the student's point of view, this means lessons that, if not identical from week to week, at least rhyme. So their teacher might, for example, work with the following:

Act 1: Welcome. Ask the student about their week, and how their practice went.

Act 2: Starting with the first assigned practice task, hear everything they were supposed to work on this week, and troubleshoot as necessary

Act 3: Based on what unfolded in Act 2, determine what's required for next week and turn that into practice instructions.

While no two lessons would have exactly the same content, students in this example studio know that the lessons usually start with a *chat*, segue into whatever they were *supposed to have worked on this week*, and then conclude with *what's ahead for next week.* If a bad practice week means they're not ready for the lesson, it's Act 2 that's going to be painful.

Of course, that's just one of many possible such templates. Another studio might prefer the following instead:

Act 1: 5 minutes of theory

Act 2: 5 minutes of scales and technical work

Act 3: 10 minutes of whatever the student is most worried about from the week of practice they just did

Act 4: 5 minutes of Random selections from what the student was supposed to have prepared, to check that they did

Act 5: 5 minutes of practice Instructions

Here these lessons have been segmented according to *time*— an idea that's absent in the previous model—as is the idea that sampling the student's work would be done *randomly*, rather than *methodically*. With 5 acts in each lesson rather than 3, this is also a model that privileges getting through a *wider range* of activities over getting through any single activity *in depth.*

I'm not holding up one model as being superior to the other; in fact, to debate the relative merits of the two would be to miss the point entirely. Not only are both these models entirely workable—despite having almost nothing in common—*there are also countless workable alternatives to both of these.*

What's interesting here is not the wealth of options, but the fact most teaching studios end up settling on one such workflow, and then sticking to it, sometimes for decades—the same way that many households end up with a favourite soap powder, or brand of toothpaste. In time, that preference cements into a *template* that will power tens of thousands of lessons, and it can be difficult to imagine that any other way of running a lesson is even possible.

The challenge here for the Dynamic Studio is not to seek the "best" usual order of attack. It's simply to be aware if you do *have* a usual order of attack, so that—every so often—you can surprise your students with a lesson that obviously hasn't read the studio script.

And I mean *really* hasn't read the studio script. I'm not talking about swapping elements around, or turning 10 minutes of theory into 5. I'm talking about where-did-*that*-come-from-we-never-do-this unexpected.

> "When have we ever started a lesson like *this?*, the student will wonder. Never; that's the point."

So one lesson, instead of starting by asking them about their week, the student might be greeted with a blank sheet of manuscript paper, and told the room is theirs for 10 minutes. Their job? To write out—from memory—as much of the first page of their new piece as they can. Key signature, time signature, tempi, dynamics, articulation marks, pitches, rhythms, the works.

The student may or may not be able to get that done, but whatever happens in that 10 minutes is going to be as fascinating for you as it was unexpected for the student. When have we ever started a lesson like *this?*, the student will wonder. Never; that's the point.

By contrast, you might run another lesson where the order of the lesson is determined by how well the student *believes* they can play particular sections of their work. The lesson begins with whatever they have most confidence in, and then gradually works its way backwards. This means that unlike regular lessons—which by their very troubleshooting nature tend to focus on whatever students are having most difficulty with—*this time you might never get to the weakest material.* What conversations and feedback might come of a lesson in which the student was spending more of their time succeeding from beginning to end?

What indeed.

And again, when parents ask students about their lesson, they'll hear "I've never had a lesson like *that* before".

Whatever order change-up you use, the message is very much "stay on your toes, you never know what's coming". You won't need to create such exceptions often; your students just need to know that they're possible, and they'll regard all their lessons in an entirely new light.

Static Studio students have a pretty good idea of what's coming, and in what order. **Dynamic Studio** students have a pretty good idea too...but are frequently very, very wrong.

(2): Shaking up your practice requests

Music teachers will often complain that students would enjoy their practice a lot more if they practiced more creatively, but if the *instructions* underpinning each week of preparation are essentially the same every time then students can hardly be blamed if their practice falls in zombie lockstep behind.

For this reason, in the battle against same-old it pays to be aware of any trends—or, worse still, *repetition*—that might be embedded in the weekly orders you give. Don't be fooled by the fact that the names of pieces and technical work seem to be changing all the time; what drives practice sessions—and where the sameness resides—are the *verbs*.

You're looking for words like **"prepare"** and **"polish"** and **"learn"** and **"speed up"**, and then noting the frequency with which each appears in your practice instructions. Leaving to one side the unhelpfully open-ended nature of such verbs (don't get me started on this, check *The Practice Revolution* if you want the full rant), what should be worrying you is how limited the list usually is.

Remember, these verbs inform what music students *do*. Send students home each week with a limited pool of verbs, and you're setting them up for repetitive, grinding practice.

What other verbs could you be using to shape their preparation time? How often, for example, do you ask them to **"watch"** a particularly good—or bad—performance on YouTube? Or **"listen"** to five very different recordings of their new piece? Or **"list"** all the dynamics, articulations and other score markings on pages 2 & 3 and then **"place"** them on a score which you have stripped of all such details? Or **"find out"** more about what was happening in the composer's life in the year that piece was written? Or **"devise"** their own fingering for a difficult passage? Or **"cement"** a fingering that you had worked out for them last lesson? Or **"brainstorm"** three completely different ways of playing the opening of their new sonata? Or **"visualize"** a performance, from beginning to end, without actually playing a note on their instrument? Or **"test drive"** their new piece in front of a dozen different family members or friends? Or **"highlight"** every instance of the entry of the subject in their fugue? Or **"record"** a note-perfect but half-speed version of the first page of the new etude, and then **"email"** it to you before the next lesson?

Here's why this is so important: *every fresh verb will prompt different behaviour from the student.* As any political scientist, marketing expert, or student of the works of George Orwell knows, there is tremendous power in the choice of words; a student asked to **"test drive"** a work will be running it from beginning to end, not stopping for red lights, because they have an audience to impress and a rehearsal to complete. By contrast, a student tasked with **"devising"** their own fingering is going to be focusing on a very small part of the piece, and thinking very technically as they do. Switch that same student to **"brainstorming"** new ways to start their Sonata, and they won't even need to be with their instrument at the time, as they switch into a highly creative what-if mode of thinking.

> *"...here's why this is so important: every fresh verb will prompt different behavior from the student."*

My own feeling is that face-to-face teaching is mostly about the choice of *adjectives*, preparation about *verbs*, while performing is about *punctuation*. You might disagree, but if it's variety you're trying to instigate, then it has to start with the instigator. You won't instigate change by keeping your requests the same.

The **Static Studio** is on the lookout for *new pieces* students could be *learning*. **Dynamic Studio** is on the lookout for *new ways* students could be *working*.

(3): Shaking up what repertoire means

For too many music teachers, "changing repertoire" means moving from page 24 to page 25 in the same book, or Book 2 to Book 3 of the same series. That's not change, that's *progression*; it delivers repertoire to students as if it were on a conveyor belt. They'll be able to see exactly what's coming up, the content of their music lessons unfolding with telegraphed karmic inevitability.

There's nothing wrong with having repertoire that logically leads students through a method or syllabus like this. There *is* something wrong if that conveyor belt is the only—or even dominant—means of delivering what-students-should-be-working-on-next. Most teachers are aware of this, and will pause the conveyor belt from time-to-time to throw something new into the mix.

But just as simply tweaking the *nouns* in practice instructions is not genuine change, simply assigning an *alternative piece* is not actually giving the student a fresh challenge. That student is still supposed to go and practice a piece until they can play it; today's computer-game savvy students will rightly not regard that as change, but as a re-skin. New graphics over the same old content. Learn a new piece. Ho hum. The only difference here is *which one*.

The dynamic alternative would be instead to periodically give them something that is not only unexpected, but doesn't even belong in the same supermarket aisle as what they've been doing so far.

So if the student has just finished Book 2, and you're looking to engage them with something new, then let's *really* make the task one they've had *no* experience in completing:

A challenge for them to relearn the piece they just did… but a *semitone higher*…or…

...a piece where you've whited out every 4th measure, and they need to learn what they *can* see, and guess what they *can't*...or...

...a piece that sets up an *artificial technical constraint* (Left hand only for piano? Pedal keyboard only for organ? A clarinet student being told they're only allowed to breathe 5 times throughout an entire adagio movement? Two performers trying to co-ordinate to perform on one violin?); constraints that means they can't take any technical skill they currently have for granted, and have to come up with brand new ways of thinking about their instrument...or...

...to prepare 5 *profoundly different interpretations* of the same piece...or...

...a *medley*, which they create, built from excerpts of every piece they've done so far this year...or...

...a piece which they need to practice with the specific aim of having the resultant performance take *exactly* 42 seconds. (Bartok would approve)...or...

...a piece which you'll actually be giving somebody else, but your student's job is to *come up with all the bowing and fingering* that they'll be using...or...

...to play a piece that another student has composed...or...

...to learn a carefully selected (not so hard) passage of an otherwise ***incredibly difficult piece*** that only the most advanced students can play. (➡ 174-175)...or...

...*Happy Birthday* for their great-grandma's upcoming 90th birthday... (they'll be playing it with a singalong audience of 200 relatives and friends), but preparing for the fact that the piano in the nursing home is 4 semitones flat, has no working pedals, a middle C that sticks, and has to be loud enough for a room full of deaf people to hear...

It doesn't matter what the difference is, as long as it's a clear example of wow-I've-never-done-*this*-before.

None of this requires abandoning methods and systemic progression—for students focused on evidence of progress, Book 3 is obviously a milestone if you've spent the rest of the year working on Book 2. But to extrapolate Robert Frost to the conclusion I always wished he'd reached, it's often when people wander *off* any sort of path entirely that they'll discover the challenges they enjoy most, work hardest to master, and remember most fondly.

The sheer impact of such unexpected requests aside, the beauty of giving students an entirely new *species* of challenge like this is that they have to develop an entirely new species of skills in response. There's a word for development like this, not delivered on rails, but evolving through unexpected opportunities: *dynamic*.

I don't know exactly what sort of lessons will result as my student turns up with those every-fourth-measure-whited-out measures filled in with what they *think* should have happened, but we'd both have a lot of fun—and learn a huge amount—finding out.

 The **Static Studio** will usually find the *next piece* on the *next page*. What the **Dynamic Studio** challenges the student with next might not even *be* a piece in the first place.

(4): Shaking up the scale of the workload

It's a rare studio that doesn't differentiate workloads to some extent by *student level*: Static Studios in particular will ensure such differentiation by encoding it into their studio policy— advanced students might be expected to do 90 minutes of practice a day, intermediate students 45 minutes, new beginners only 15.

The logic is that by having a quota like this, the studio guarantees a workable minimum of lesson preparation.

Apart from the awful unintended consequences that such time-based practice brings (again, *The Practice Revolution* rails against this in detail), the problem here is the very constancy of the demands. It's like jogging on a completely flat circuit: no downhills for *respites*; no uphills for *challenges*. If you're an intermediate student, then that means 45 minutes a day, every day, rain, hail or whatever; practicing takes on a mantra-like quality, each session being a countdown-timed doppelganger of the session before.

This is not preparation. This is a *chore*, as regular, predictable and grey-sky dull as hanging clothes on a line.

The Dynamic Studio views practice requirements somewhat differently; not as a vehicle for mandatory minimums, but as both a variable and a motivational tool in its own right. Like the *content* of practice sessions, or the *nature* of assigned repertoire, how *hard* students are expected to push themselves is something that would be fluid; partly to accommodate the peaks and troughs created by the student's other nonmusical commitments, but also to keep the journey unpredictable and engaging.

So, for example, the Dynamic Studio will sometimes hit students with an *unexpected hill*: a task that normally would require extended preparation, but due in a fraction of that time.

A performance, for example, scheduled in a fortnight, of a piece they're seeing for the very first time today(!)

Or the teacher will set not a floor, but a *ceiling*: the student might have a *maximum* of 2 hours of practice to complete the task set, and not one second more—the challenge then for the student is not about *passing their required practice time*, but *extracting as much as possible from every second*.

Two different challenges. Two *completely* different practice weeks and workloads in response.

Or the student might be thanked for the excellent work they've done so far this semester, and then *given a week off*. For many music teachers—brought up with the belief that practice has to be *every day* or somewhere a music fairy dies—the idea of a week off is heresy, but the motivating power of an unexpected break is something that elite sports coaches are thoroughly familiar with. (This is not the book for me to rant about it, but don't believe a *word* of You Must Practice Every Day. It's utter nonsense.)

> "For many music teachers—brought up with the belief that practice has to be *every day* or somewhere a music fairy dies—the idea of a week off is heresy"

Or they might have their workload scaled not by *time* requirements or constraints, but by the size and demands of a *checklist* that the student has to get through during the week. Instead of the usual half dozen items, they might be hit with a 2 page monster list, and the promise of a reward if they can get through it all—however long that takes.

Double workloads, practice caps rather than floors, weeks off, checklist marathons, unexpected and imminent performances...

who saw any of *that* coming? How can students be left feeling that lessons are an endless grind of deadline preparations when such landmarks are surprise features on the practice landscape?

Of course, the unexpected respites are not just there because you're being kind: it's much easier for you to ask students to dial things up when it's really needed if occasionally you've been prepared to make unsolicited concessions when it's not. It helps students to view you not as a taskmaster who values industry for busyness's sake, but as a strategist who is actually helping them get the most possible from their time.

And it will help keep students who are grindstone-weary from leaving because of the relentless—and often entirely arbitrary—pressure that accompanies a fixed workload.

The **Static Studio** maintains *a steady workload*, that's character building and unyielding. The **Dynamic Studio** periodically tips the scales to create *respites* and *challenges*.

(5): Shaking up targets

Most studios are very clear about what students are working towards; the idea is that students who are focused on a goal will be more motivated. I have no issue with this—to teach without goalsetting is to teach crippled.

What is an issue is when those goals become monolithic.

In Australia most music students are working towards graded **examinations**, with the exam itself becoming the big annual focal point for the lessons. Almost everything assigned, practiced and taught is framed by that, and it inevitably produces a syllabus and outcomes driven approach to lessons. This is not necessarily a bad thing, nor does it stop teachers from introducing elements outside of the system—it's just that there's often simply not time. You can quite easily keep your entire studio very busy simply by focusing on examinations and nothing else; it won't come as a galloping shock to anyone reading this book that I therefore very rarely prepare students for exams.

Elsewhere in the world—and for teachers in Australia not interested in exams—studios are sometimes driven instead by **competitions,** with repertoire being determined by this year's set pieces; others revolve around **regular studio recitals**; yet others around **progressing through a series of books.**

Now before the protests start, most studios of course work with a *blend* of these motivating entities, but focus will normally still be heavily stacked each year in favour of the same few opportunities or landmark events.

The problem comes about if such landmarks reach a point where they're the raison d'être for your entire studio. With all your motivational eggs then in one basket (or even two or three baskets) students who are not fired up by whatever that focus is will fail to be fired up at all—and you'll lose them.

Worse still, *almost all of these traditional focus events are based around preparing for performance of some type*, which means that they differ from each other only in detail.

There are many, many more alternatives to whatever you currently have students working towards than you might think—including many different alternatives to traditional performance-focused goals. Since it's your studio, you're completely free to work with any, several, all or none of these options; you're also free to *engineer* brand new focuses that you might never have used before, and that—apart from *this one student*, for whom it's *perfect*—you might never use again.

A wider world of lesson targets

We'll look in much more detail in the next chapter at some of the alternatives there are to the traditional learn-*this-piece*-so-you-can-perform-it-on-*this-date* model that fuels so many music lessons. But even within the confines of that model, there are plenty of variations that are not so commonly used, and which students may just find intriguing. To get a sense of some of these options, the next time you go to a music teacher conference, talk to as many teachers as you can, and ask them what it is that their studio has students preparing for; you'll hear a lot of the same-old, but in the mix will also be some engaging possibilities that you might never have considered.

So alongside reports of studio recitals and competitions you might hear about a studio that has every student *making their own annual recording*; another that *posts videos* of performances of each completed piece to the studio website; another that has students *composing pieces* for each other; another that pits teams of students against each other in a *repertoire accumulation* contest; yet another that doesn't have en-masse studio recitals, but instead has each student organising their own *private mini-recital*, to which they invite family and friends.

Yet another might indeed work towards "exams", but using a syllabus that the teacher created, rather than something determined by a distant committee. (This is very much what I do for my own martial arts students)

Or another that combines with other studios to create biannual themed festivals: this one focusing on *sightreading*, the next on *ensemble works*, the one after that on *music from the movies*.

Or another that has students *recording their piece every week*—warts and all, wherever it happens to be up to—with the focus not being on how it *eventually* ends up sounding, but how it is *developing*, in much the same way that clients of building projects sometimes review time-lapse photography of progress, from foundations to lockup stage.

> "...these are not just different *goals* for students; they also represent *completely different ways of working*"

What's important with all this variety is that these are not just different goals for students; they also represent completely different ways of working, both in the studio, and at home.

So, for example:

Students **making their own recording** need to be even more fastidious about *detail*, because the performance is being captured for all time, but don't need to be as concerned about *deadlines*, because the recording can be made whenever they're ready. Their lessons will be tougher on missing the occasional articulation mark, more relaxed about getting everything done by the first Saturday in April.

Students **preparing a private mini-recital** don't have to be concerned about possibly playing the *same piece* as lots of other students (which is agony at a studio recital), but will need to have *more pieces ready to go*, so that their big show is not over after 90 seconds.

Students **working in teams** where the goal is as-many-pieces-as-possible for the repertoire accumulation contest are going to be *practicing* very differently from students who only have three pieces to get ready in the next six months, but are being assessed by an examiner at the end of that time; it's not unreasonable to assume that the former will end up with *better reading skills*, the latter, with *more polished and secure performances*.

Students who work towards **biannual festivals** where the themes are always changing will end up with a *broader range* of skills after a few years of lessons, at the expense of having covered any one of those skills in depth.

What might lessons look like if you were to open up new goals for your students, beyond those to which you've been faithful for all these years? How would those changes flow through into lessons, into the pacing of expectations, into the preparation students need to do at home? Which students might find the new way of working a better match to their own particular skills and weaknesses? What new repertoire might be introduced into the studio? What new opportunities for students to shine?

And which musical or developmental issues might your studio actually be doing a better job with—or working seriously on for the very first time?

The **Static Studio** *points students* towards existing goalposts.
The **Dynamic Studio** *creates goalposts* with specific students in mind.

(6): Shaking up your Studio layout

Not all Dynamic Studio changes are about the way you relate to students, or the nature of the instructions and goals you assign. One powerful way to change the rhythm of lessons—without actually *declaring* any changes at all—is to simply redefine the space in which the lessons take place.

Any store fitout expert will confirm that the layout of your business space sends a message; if your studio looks much as it did ten years ago, then the message in this case would be that *nothing changes.* That might be reassuring if you're a bank, but it's a terrible signal to be sending music students, however subliminally.

The quickest way to break out of a layout rut like this is not to waste time overthinking alternatives, but just to start swapping items in your studio around, like scrabble tiles on a rack. For reasons we'll look at in a moment, you really can't go wrong: short of piling all your furniture hard against the front door, almost every change brings with it opportunities for fresh perspectives—and new teaching possibilities.

So. Take a deep breath. Look around your studio. Now let's mess everything up, then think through what the changes might *mean.*

The new layout: some possibilities

The hardest part of rethinking layout is disregarding what's already there: it can be difficult to imagine alternatives when items seem to "belong" in particular spaces. So the immediate battle is about trying to see the space as if it were empty, and you were starting over—take a moment to picture that, and now unleash the what if's...

What would happen if all the furniture in the room faced in a new direction, so that what used to be the *front* of the room is now the *back?* Or if your own teaching chair was much closer to your students? Or much further away? Or if you faced parents while you teach, instead of teaching with your back to them?

If you have a piano, does it sound better or worse if it's up the other end of the room? Or in the center of the room? Or hard up against a wall? Does that bookshelf make a good backdrop for the student as they play? Or does it actually distract them, and is better off out of sight? Is it something that you regularly need to access, but is nowhere near where you sit? Would your lessons flow better, with less time wasted rummaging, if the resources on that shelf were *alphabetized*? Or sorted by *how advanced* the students were? Or by *which day of the week* you're likely to need them?

> "...the layout of your business space sends a message; if your studio looks much as it did ten years ago, then the message would be that *nothing changes.*"

What would happen if your studio walls were covered with thought-provoking, imagination-stimulating images and quotes? Or if they were completely *stripped* so that the room had a minimalist feel, with just you, the student, and their music stand? Or covered with photos of your students, past and present, with news and testimonials? Or whiteboards? Or oversized calendars highlighting everything that's coming up in the next 18 months? Or honor boards, featuring the names of practice champions, students of the month, best new students, Audience Choice Awards at recitals, competition winners, together with brand new boards, with headings yet to be determined?

What if that music stand faced a different direction, not permanently, but rotating like a weather vane *depending on what was being worked on in the lesson?* So if it's facing the mirror, then the focus is *posture*. Turned to face the window, then the focus is *beautiful phrasing*. Facing the wall with the big poster that says DETAILS!, then the student will be *trawling the score* for articulation and dynamic markings they may have missed. Or facing the rest of the room, with the lights dimmed, then it's time for a *playthrough* under *performance conditions*.

Mockup performance ambience aside, what happens if you replace the central ceiling light with a couple of lamps, and actually had substantially *less* lighting in the studio? Or—for your sleepy late afternoon students—much *more* light? Or had *coloured* lights that you could switch between, to change the type of thinking the student should be doing (blue: List *positives*; Yellow: Find a *completely new way to play the same passage*; Red: List *problems to fix*; Green: turn off the part of your brain that assesses or criticises and *just play*)

What happens if your student were to have a few lessons where they were expected to play *sitting down*, rather than standing up? Or while *walking around?* What fresh conversations might the new perspective prompt? How differently might they regard balance, stability and posture when sanity is restored?

…as with many of the ideas for change in this chapter, it's not the *what* that's important so much as the fact that there *is* change. If you get stuck, start by *actually* taking everything out of your studio, and working with the blank canvas—you'll be amazed how many ideas you end up with as you bring the items back in…

…and by how many items you might decide not to bring back in at all, and what might replace them instead. (See the chapter on Dynamic Resourcing (➡²53) for some ideas on *that*)

Change the space, change the behaviour

Reinventing the workspace is not just about better first impressions and an injection of "here's-something-different". Even seemingly insignificant changes in your workspace can have marked flow-on effects on *how* you work.

So, for example, if you rearrange the room so that you're now sitting nowhere near your student, you won't be making physical corrections anywhere near as often as you used to. Or writing so often on the music they're reading from. You'll be *less likely* to notice problems with how they position their fingers, but *more likely* to notice problems with posture. You'll have a different perspective on the *sound* they're producing. You might not be able to see exactly where they're looking as they play; you might also find yourself *watching* less, and *listening* a little harder. With you now also not literally looking over their shoulder, the student might play with *more freedom*...or *less*, if you now seem to them more like an audience, or a jury, way back in your new chair.

All significant changes to how you teach, flowing from an apparently trivial change to the teaching environment. Any classroom teacher will confirm immediately the power of this principle; it's the reason that so many will come in during their holidays to change things around, as they fuss about getting this Just Right for the semester ahead.

Whatever configuration they settle on, you can be sure of this: it almost certainly won't be the same as *last* semester.

You can easily click "undo"

These changes don't need to last long to have the effect you need, and so any inconvenience inherent in the new arrangement can be short-lived. By then though, the new layout will have worked its magic twice: the first time with it's studio-wide injection of "wow, what's this???" when you switched to the new layout, and then again when you switched *back*, when the return to your "old" studio layout will feel like coming home again after a vacation. It's old, it's familiar, but it's no longer tired.

If you decide to keep the new layout though, make a note of the date, then set yourself an alarm in (say) a year's time. Your studio makeover may be New and Fresh and Awesome right now, but it's the very newness that is necessary for the awesome: as the new wears off, the awesome will steadily deflate to "useful" and then "adequate" and then "ho hum"; your job is to reinvent it again before it starts to smell.

This is one of these put-the-book-down-now-and-just-*try*-it ideas; you'll be glad you did. It's not just your students who will come out of it feeling recharged.

A decade of photos of the **Static Studio** will be hard to distinguish from each other. A decade of photos of a **Dynamic Studio** would be impossible to play snap with.

(7): Shaking up the extent of parental involvement

It's not talked about nearly often enough, but nothing limits or frees what's possible in a lesson quite like the decision over whether parents sit in. Unfortunately, all too often this too is determined simply by inertia: parents who historically have sat in will usually continue to do so; those who have dropped-and-run in the past will probably drop-and-run in the future.

The problem here is that the crucial decision over sitting in is not made after a careful examination of the impact on the lesson, or the child, or any of the relationships involved, but by an appeal to *tradition*. The mere fact that the parent is *used* to sitting in—or not—is sufficient to ensure that they continue to.

A much more interesting question is less descriptive, more normative: not "what has this parent's sit-in behaviour been so far", but "*should* this parent be sitting-in in the future"?

One illuminating exercise is to run experiments: be open with parents about the fact that you're trying to figure out how— or even whether—they should be involved each week, then start test driving the possibilities. Your experiments will mean that you'll be trying lessons with:

Parent(s) not just in the room, but actively *taking notes;*

Parent(s) there, but *occupied* reading;

Parent(s) there for *part* of the lesson;

Parent(s) *dropping-and-running.*

I've put the plural in brackets each time, because it's also worth assessing the impact of *which* parent is involved—invite sometimes one, sometimes the other, sometimes both.

Whichever variation happens to be in play for the lesson then, your job is to watch the student very closely, and note any behaviour changes. How much easier or harder is it to have them *follow directions?* How much more or less *open to new suggestions* are they? Do they *laugh* more easily? *Chat* more reluctantly? *Look at the clock* every two minutes, instead of not at all? *Look to their parent(s)* for approval before they do anything? More or less inclined to *misbehave?* And—and this is a huge indicator of whether parents should be anywhere near the lesson—are they more or less *willing to make mistakes?*

Run your tests. Note the results. It might take you half a dozen lessons to test-drive the various combinations, but then in the following semester, you can adopt—on a semi-permanent basis—a lesson sitting in recommendation that's not founded on here's-how-we've-done-this-so-far, but grounded in what has effectively been *research*, and tailored to the individual student.

Note *recommendation*, and note *semi*-permanent. You're not mandating anything, and the central point this chapter is trying to make is that no matter how well thought-through a policy is, it's the occasional exceptions that will keep your lessons feeling fresh. So even if parents are much better off *in* the room—because the student tends to behave like a gremlin that's been fed and watered after midnight otherwise—it's worth still having a lesson every so often with parents waiting in the car. The only thing that's certain about the lesson that follows is that it will be *different* than it would have been otherwise; for the purposes of a teacher seeking to ensure that lessons don't start to become indistinguishable from each other, that's mission accomplished.

> "...nothing limits or frees what's possible in a lesson quite like the decision over whether parents sit in."

The **Static Studio** has parents sitting in—or not—according to whether they always have. The **Dynamic Studio** treats whether parents sit in or not as a variable to be *optimized.*

---

(8): Shaking up your schedule

The subject of *scheduling* is actually surprisingly fertile and has a chapter in its own right (➡93), not least because there are few objects in the known universe subject to such inertia as a music student's lesson time. Given how painful it can be to orchestrate the A-goes-to-B-who-goes-to-C-who-replaces-A swaps, unless there is a clash of monumental proportions, most teachers will resist lesson time changes the way most nations would resist a change to their borders.

But this means that a student who you work with at 4pm on a Friday is someone you've probably only ever seen at the *end of a school day*, at the *very end of a week*. How different might lessons be—how different might the *student* be—if the lesson was earlier in the day, or on a Saturday?

What might an early evening lesson be like? Or an early morning? Do you know *anybody* who would present the same for all of those times?

And perhaps more to the point, do *you* present the same at all those times? What are you like for the students who turn up first thing in the morning? Do you tend to be more energised then? More forgiving? More or less talkative? Too sleepy to be picking up little mistakes? Do you have a doppelganger who teaches the evenings who is almost the opposite? Which of your students might benefit from a little dose of that Other You?

This has always been very much an issue in my own teaching studio, and can definitely make the difference between students staying and not. I'm one of these lucky people who only needs 4-5 hours of sleep a night, so I usually have twice the energy levels of whoever is stumbling into the room for a 7am lesson. This lends itself well to a particular type of lesson where I am driving everything that happens; the student can be half asleep, but still be propelled forward by a somewhat caffeinated and let's-go style of teaching. This works brilliantly for some students, and leaves them feeling energised for the day ahead, but leaves others simply feeling like they've been run over by a truck.

Evening lessons by contrast are usually much calmer and more reflective, better suited to a more conversational-style of lesson, longer works, and more advanced students.

With the lesson time having a bearing on the type of lesson that ensues, keeping these variations in mind when scheduling has a huge bearing on my ability to keep students. Students who don't want to be run over at 7am often find the more Socratic approach of evening classes more to their liking; likewise those students who would rather just be told what to do are better off coming in the morning.

Reality is not quite as bipolar as this probably reads, but you would be a rare teacher indeed if your 8am lessons have the same flavour as those in your 8pm timeslots.

However carefully you tailor timeslots though, it's worth occasionally and temporarily rescheduling a student to a lesson at the other end of the day, or a different part of the week—you'll be surprised by how often the student will ask whether the change could be made permanent. (Of course it can. As long as "permanent" means "with occasional exceptions to keep things fresh").

The **Static Studio** knows a great lesson time is one where the student has *no colliding calendar entries*. The **Dynamic Studio** knows that *square pegs* still don't fit in *round holes*, even if both the peg and the hole happen to be free at that time.

(9): Shaking up your resources

In the same way that introducing new targets for your students adds much more than the mere presence of additional goals, introducing a new teaching resource into the studio doesn't just add equipment: it adds *brand new ways to spend the half hour that is their lesson.*

There's an entire chapter devoted to Dynamic Resourcing later in the book (➡ 253), but what's important to understand here is the transformative impact even seemingly unremarkable additions to your studio can have—let's take a look at just one example:

One modest new tool; countless new options

As studio resources go, there's nothing particularly spectacular about a *whiteboard*. It's not high-tech, expensive, or exotic— your students will have seen plenty of whiteboards before.

But if they've never seen one in your *studio* before, then its sudden introduction has the potential to be a huge rhythm changer, particularly if you're prepared to mess with your students' heads a little as they're meeting your new toy for the first time.

Picture it from the students' point of view: in of itself, the introduction of a whiteboard would be moderately interesting, simply because it's new. What would make it *fascinating* though is if you've gone almost the whole lesson without telling them what it's for...despite the fact that written on it is something utterly compelling...

...their *name.*

Wait a minute, they'll be thinking...that's *me.* Why am I up there?

What's going *on* today?

As is the case with any new resource, this studio addition is doing some of its best work even when it's not in active use, simply by keeping the Curiosity Particles Per Million count (CPPM) dangerously high.

So what is this whiteboard ultimately for? It actually doesn't matter. You might be using it for your student to do some *rhythmic dictation* at the end of the lesson. Or for you to write a big *score* out of 10 for how well prepared you thought they were. Or for you both to run a *scales game* that turns the whiteboard into a game of *battleships*. Or for your student to draw a curve that represents their intended *changes in dynamics* over time in their new piece, over which you can then chart the dynamics they're *actually* producing.

Or on which you will be drawing—Pictionary style, without saying a single word—*all feedback* you give in this lesson. (try it! It's a lesson neither of you will forget: the student has to do all the talking to zero in on exactly what you mean, and in the process, will be absorbing your recommendations like never before).

The exact use to which you put your new resource is not what's important here. What is important is that it's very *presence* was unexpected, the student left guessing. Your lessons may well ordinarily have a certain rhythm; today though, that's been disrupted as surely as if it had been defibrillated.

We'll look later in the book at many more examples of studio resources, and how best to make use of them (➡️²⁵³), but one of the strengths of a writeable medium like a whiteboard is the extent to which it *retains* its novelty value, as it can be *erased*, and new things written. Which means that next week, when the student is reading something completely different on there, it gets to work its magic all over again. Maybe this time the whiteboard lists not just their name, but **their name and someone else's**.

What does that pair of names *mean*, they'll wonder. What do you *want* it to mean? Perhaps this is a way of introducing a *duet pairing.* Or their assigned *rival* in the upcoming practice competition. Or maybe they're a *team* for the same competition. Or maybe the other name is one of your senior students who will be their *mentor* in the next semester. Or the name of a beginner student they will be mentor*ing*. Or the names of the two students last week who were *students of the week.* (Hey look! You're one of them!) Or the name of the student they need to create a *key signature theory question* for...and answer a question set by them.

Again, if the student is left to imagine all the possibilities for a good portion of the lesson, the final answer almost doesn't matter. And then when you're done, before next week's lesson, you get to erase the whiteboard, and put something up there again. (It then says "**Countdown: 51 days**....ok, *now* what's going on?")

Are you suddenly a better teacher because of the addition of the whiteboard? Probably not. Are your students more engaged in the lesson? Absolutely. Which means they'll already be looking forward a little more to *next* week.

If you're wondering now what you need to go and buy, then you're missing the point: your home is *already filled* with items that your students have never seen and are perfect teaching props.

The **Static Studio** daydreams about *new equipment* to help them get the most from their *lessons.* The **Dynamic Studio** daydreams about *new lessons* to help them get the most from their *equipment.*

What's next:

This chapter has been deliberately less about dramatic change, more about unsettling established patterns, with examples of circuit-breakers that are actually carefully designed to *accommodate* and *complement* the way you already do things.

For teachers who want to follow the rabbit-hole a little deeper, the more you're prepared to let go of what you've been used to, the more possibilities open up. The next chapter poses an unsettling question that few Static Studios ever dare ask themselves, because the answers can make traditional music lessons seem a little, well, *thin*...

The Diversified Studio

What computer game developers understand
that music teachers don't

The Diversified Studio

GIVEN THE EXTRAORDINARY TIME COMMITMENT AND opportunity cost music lessons represents for students, families are inevitably going to be regularly assessing whether it's all worth it; there's nothing "soft" or "uncommitted" about this—it's simply common sense on their part.

The very best defence a music teacher can have against such assessments going *badly* is to be regularly asking themselves a confronting question:

Just what is there for students in your studio to *do?*

Now just bear with me for a moment. I'm aware that this question sounds pointlessly self-evident. What is there for students to *do?* Are you *kidding?* These are *music lessons...*what do you *think* there is for students to do?...

But it's an entirely serious question, with implications for everything you might be thinking about adding, editing or removing from your current studio, and you can't answer it meaningfully by simply restating your job's title. So I'll ask again—because, I promise you, *students and parents will be asking themselves down the track:*

What is there for students in your studio to *do?*

OK. So. Obviously there's lessons to attend, recitals to show up to, practice to get done, competitions to enter. But beyond that—beyond the everyday stuff of simply having lessons, practicing in the six days between, and then performing whatever has been worked on—what else is there in your studio to keep students engaged and coming back?

If the answer now seems a little thin—particularly if, on reflection, you realise that really the *only* thing on offer is what's immediately related to the lessons themselves—then you've got all your student retention eggs in one basket. As soon as anything goes wrong with those core lessons (and at some point something will) the student has no reason to stay. Wavering parents will have That Conversation with each other, and then with you—we've all been there, and it's not a great feeling.

> "...beyond the everyday stuff of simply having lessons, what else is there in your studio to keep students engaged and coming back?"

The word to describe every-thing you're about to read is *diver-sification*, which sounds horribly Business-Degree-dry, but really all it means is extending your studio's offerings so that mem-bership of your studio can mean much, much more than just weekly lessons. You can use the existence of these new options both as a point of differentiation to entice prospective students, and—most importantly—to give the students you already have additional reasons to continue the adventure.

The result is not just that you'll end up with a much longer answer to the what-is-there-for-students-in-your-studio-to-do question, but a studio that is genuinely unlike any other in town, with—and this is key—*more activities to be part of than any single student could ever get through.*

This breadth of offerings then means that if students are starting to grow weary of a studio activity they're currently enrolled in, they can switch to another activity and *still stay in your studio.* This gives you a huge advantage over Static studios that offer traditional-weekly-lessons-only: the only way their students can meaningfully change what they're doing is to *leave.*

Interestingly, this particular Dynamic Studio strategy is a client retention technique sampled directly from a multi-billion dollar industry that has nothing whatsoever to do with music lessons. Let's take a moment to see how it works.

Learning lessons from MMORPGs

You might not be familiar with the acronym, but MMORPG stands for Massively Multiplayer Online Role Playing Game, and they have been a phenomenon that have helped transform the computer game industry into a behemoth that has now overtaken the movie industry as the #1 mass-entertainment vehicle on the planet.

What's interesting for music teachers here—and the reason it should be considered compulsory professional development for every music teacher to try one of these games at least once—is that these games are not something you just buy; they're something you *subscribe* to. Once the subscription stops, your access to the game stops, but so does that income stream for the game's publisher. This means that the companies that produce such games are under enormous pressure to keep on coming up with fresh reasons for players to stay subscribed.

> "It's not just variety for variety's sake: it's a compelling and growing list of reasons to *stay*."

And they've become very, very good at it.

So to take the most successful of these early MMORPGS—the venerable (and infamous) *World of Warcraft*—there is simply an *astonishing* range of things to do. Players who want to go on **epic quests** and **slay monsters** can do that, of course. But the game also caters for players who want to indulge in **archeology**, exploring the game world for rare artifacts, and then assembling them into **collectable items**. Or players who like the thrill of responding to real-time price fluctuations in the **in-game auction house,** buying virtual items cheaply, waiting until events in the game produce a spike in demand, and then selling them at a profit. Or players who like to take on the most overwhelming and **technically challenging boss fights** in the game, risking group wipeouts for the most powerful rewards. Or players who enjoy cultivating a reputation of excellence among other players, and who spend time turning themselves into a **master blacksmith,** or **tailor,** or **alchemist,** with services for hire. Or players who like to **compete** with other players in organised **team-based virtual sports**. Or players who like to **explore the world** for rare minerals or herbs. Or players who don't want to fight monsters, but will accompany and **heal** the wounds of those who do. Or players who like to **organise and motivate** other people, founding Guilds, sharing resources and expertise to defeat challenges that are impossible for single players. Or players who like to methodically work their way through the thousands of **official Achievements** there are to earn in-game...

...the point here is that there is actually more to do than any single person could ever do in a lifetime of playing the game, and the game's developers are constantly adding more.

So why would a music teacher care about this?

Because the sheer scale of this smorgasbord of possible activities is no accident, nor is it just variety for variety's sake: *it's a compelling and growing list of reasons to stay*, even when the core reasons that brought the player to the game in the first place have been exhausted. And stay they do—in the millions—often for many, many hours every day.

Running wide as well as running deep

Out of the box, music studios are not at all ready to adopt anything even vaguely resembling the World of Warcraft diversity model. Most music studios are focused on *depth*; on being able to take beginners as far as they possibly can; on layering musical skills and techniques in the same bottom-up methodical and relentless way a mathematician builds from basic counting through to calculus and beyond. This is not out of blind deference to tradition: excellence demands depth.

But retaining today's students demands more. More than ever before retaining students now also demands *breadth*. A studio that has exciting and varied answers to the question "so... what else is there?" is much better placed to keep students should the gloss of the core lessons be fading.

Remember, like a MMORPG, our clients are effectively subscribers. They subscribe for a term, or semester, or whatever your studio policy requires, but at the end of each of those units of time they're free to *un*subscribe. As any game developer will tell you, it's not enough to *remove all the reasons to leave*; you have to actively *create reasons to stay*. The key is to make sure that list of reasons to stay is *long*, and regularly being *added to*.

So what could your studio be offering students beyond mere music lessons? This chapter looks at 14 different examples, most structured as addons which students can *elect* to be part of, and that run in parallel to your regular traditional lessons. So they'd have their weekly lesson, but their fees also entitles them to participation in special extra classes that you might hold on (say) the 1st and 3rd Tuesday of every month; classes in...

...well, that's the thing. It's your studio. You get to choose. Let's sample some possibilities:

Extension Option 1: Whose note is it anyway?

Students who have been taking part in this studio extension will be easy to spot at your studio recitals, because right there in front of a hall full of parents and students, they'll be making up their pieces on the spot(!)

To get them to that point though, they will have been taking part in many, many intensive sessions as part of a special Improvisation program that you've set up—almost certainly the only one of its kind in town.

It's beyond the scope of this book to provide a Comprehensive Guide To Running Improv

> "...no matter what you think your own limitations are as an improviser, you'll still quickly be astonished by what your *students* are able to do (which is the point)"

Classes, but the condensed version is to start with drills that are simple enough that every student is able to cope, and then ramp it up from there.

So, for example, every student can succeed immediately if the only instruments on hand in that very first improvisation session are basic percussion instruments, for *rhythm-only* improvs. Or whatever sounds they can make with their voices. Or whatever notes they like on their own instrument, as long as it's one of *these* notes in the pentatonic scale, using *this* rhythmic pattern. Great. Now make up your *own* pattern. Now let's make up your own pattern *and* dynamics. Let's try it again, same idea, different dynamics. Now all staccatissimo. Excellent, now this time legatissimo, and you're only allowed to change to a new note 5 times altogether in the two minutes...choose carefully...

A month or so after that, and you might have them deconstructing "Chopsticks"—no matter what instrument they actually play—and then starting to make up simple parts to go over the top.

Ahead, all sorts of possibilities open up. Basic blues. Performances from fake books, or figured bass parts. Or a progression you gave them just minutes earlier. Or a progression *they* came up with just minutes earlier. Or I-start-the-tune, you-finish-it. Or a piece built from a handful of random notes that someone in the audience calls out. Or come up with chords to support *this* melody. Or their own variations on *Twinkle Twinkle Little Star*. Or a duel, between two of your most capable improvisers, each trying to outdo each other in a series of ever-more-outlandish question and answer phrases...

It's up to you, and if you layer it like this, no matter what you think your own limitations are as an improviser, you'll still quickly be astonished by what your *students* are able to do (which is the point). Not all students will shine, but those who do will be the talking point of your next recital...and prompt plenty of new signups to your new club.

As with any extension you might consider, you don't need to be handling all this in their regular lessons; instead, it might be that every second Monday they've been getting together with you and jamming across a range of styles, together with occasional club outings to workshops held by jazz musicians, composers and even Theatre Sports experts (think *Whose Line Is It Anyway?*). These students are still having their regular lessons as well, but this ability to just sit down and *play*—no music required—adds a whole new dimension...and fresh reasons to continue lessons for years to come.

Extension Option 2: Hardcore Sightreading

Again, these students will stand out at your recitals—they're not making up their piece, but they are performing it *while seeing it for the very first time.* If you really want to astonish, program an *ensemble* of such students—a string quartet, or piano duet, sight unseen.

While you may also elect to run a similar club for those who simply want to gently *improve* their sightreading, the aim of the Hardcore Sightreading Club is very much to take students who already have reasonable sightreading skills, and develop those skills to insane levels of proficiency. When the club meets, you'd be taking them through advanced sightreading techniques and tactics, but mostly they'd be neck-deep in examples that they'd be trying themselves.

The single biggest reason most students struggle with sightreading is because there was never the time available to make it strong...

> "...How much quicker might they progress in the future, with so little of their practice time now having to be about *decoding* new pieces?"

what if, just once, instead of dedicating another hundred hours to preparing a new piece for Yet Another Performance, the student signs up for your Hardcore Sightreading Club and spent the same amount of time fast-tracking their reading? How much quicker might they progress in the future, with so little of their practice time now having to be about *decoding* new pieces, and more about actually *playing* them?

And what impression will your studio create among students and colleagues from other studios, as the sightreading strengths of your own students consistently shines in cross-studio rehearsals...to say nothing of the legendary Seeing The Piece For The First Time performances that happen at your recitals?

As for each of the 14 ideas listed here, all this is possible if you set up the program. None of it is possible if you don't; it's your studio, you get to decide what to astonish people with :)

The **Static Studio** trains musicians who are able—given time—to prepare performances. The **Dynamic Studio** trains musicians who are also able to simply *play*, with no preparation necessary.

Extension Option 3: Club Impossible

There's a well-worn saying: if you aim for the stars and fall short, you might still get to the moon...

...students who sign up for your Impossible Club do so knowing that they will be given challenges that might sound all but unattainable, but are then supported by—and accountable to—other club members as they work towards that goal. It's a chance for your most ambitious and capable students to stretch each other; it's also an opportunity for underperforming but able students to lift.

And for your studio as a whole, it's a chance to oversee some truly extraordinary projects.

The range of challenges is completely open ended; there's no reason to expect that any year in the program will resemble any other. So one student might be tasked with recording an entire set of etudes. Another might undertake to perform to a total of 10,000 people; contacting schools, community groups, nursing homes, festivals, hospitals, to work through the total, a hundred or so at a time. Yet another might be challenged to perform a different duet with each student in the studio. Another might elect to arrange, rehearse and perform the first movement of Beethoven's 7th Symphony with five other students. Yet another might be working to produce their own book of beginner's pieces, complete with illustrations and recordings. Another might be taking on assisting the music director for a local school musical. Or *being* the musical director.

Your job here? Coach. Motivator. Mentor. Facilitator. Finding the words that lift them when they're low; celebrating their triumphs, pushing them to go further than they—or their parents—ever thought possible. From a job-satisfaction perspective, this option certainly beats Teaching Book 3 Yet Again: run your own Club Impossible for a while and you will be part of some truly memorable adventures, and quite possibly, some headlines.

The **Static Studio's** student achievements are much the same, year after year. The **Dynamic Studio** student achievements are as unpredictable as they are astounding.

Extension Option 4: Stylemasters

A lot of teaching repertoire is somewhat genre agnostic, with representative elements from a vast array of styles appearing throughout the books as if there are quotas to fill: on page three, something that sounds vaguely bluesy; on page 4, a minuet;

page 5 is country and western...I think...because it's called "The Lonesome Cowboy" and there's a picture of a banjo, but otherwise who can tell(?)...; page 6 is filled with whole tone scales and has a vaguely Monet-looking picture of a haystack above its French title.

Hmmm. You don't need to be a hardened musicologist to worry that this is perhaps paddling in a very shallow end of a short pool. (I think "puddle" is the word I'm looking for)

The idea behind Genre Explorer clubs is to go beyond these fleeting samplers and give students a more thorough—and most importantly, *usable*—understanding of some of these different genres. So if you're going to do **Country and Western**, then really do it: students would leave the club not just having once played a piece with "Lonesome Cowboy" in the title, but having reverse-engineered dozens of celebrated works in the genre— the progressions, the melodies, the lyrics, the instrumentation, the performance conventions—and then not just performed works of their own, but used virtual instruments on the studio computer to create their own plausible backing tracks. (➡️255)

In another semester, you might instead be studying **impressionism**, with all students who sign up working in depth on Debussy, Ravel, Delius, Satie, Scriabin...combined with excursions to art galleries to complement the music with studies of impressionist painters. The whole thing might culminate in releasing a recording of student performances, or a special concert, or a group booking to a recital by a master performer of impressionist works. The result is a very different experience and depth of understanding from students who otherwise had only ever played that Haystack whole tone piece on page 6.

Taking this approach of rotating to a new genre every 3-6 months, you might in turn tackle atonal music, or Latin Jazz, or film scores, or minimalism, or themes and variations...students who are in your studio for several years would then leave with a workable familiarity with a range of styles.

Alternatively, you might decide to have just one such expansion style that would be a studio speciality, and that runs in perpetuity: if your own background is such that you have particular expertise in classical rather than jazz saxophone repertoire, then that's what your ongoing workshops would focus on. Your studio would then be known not just for its excellent teaching, but as *the* place to go to work on such repertoire.

There's another benefit to running such classes: your intake doesn't have to be limited to those students you teach regularly; these clubs become more valuable for your studio—and more useful to the participants—if they also attracted interested students from other studios, and if reciprocation from colleagues means that your students in turn are able to access genres that go beyond your immediate area of expertise. Any student who is a member of any of the studios in the network is welcome to attend any such Stylemasters session.

So lessons with you still means regular music lessons, but it also means so much more—it might be what unlocks participation in a Power Ballad songwriting course with one of your colleagues. So be it.

The **Static Studio** ensures students get a *taste* of a wide range of musical styles and genres. The **Dynamic Studio** aims to turn such samples into genuine *proficiencies*.

Extension Option 5: Power Practice Skills

There is nothing more destructive to music lessons than problems with practice; yet there are also few issues in all of music that teachers give less help for. I've grumped at length about the dangers of this most fundamental of oversights in my other books, but one of the common complaints I hear in response is that there simply isn't time in lessons to give students the practice help they need.

That's fine. So don't handle it during lessons. Set up regular practice skills workshops instead, where students come not to learn to *play*, but to learn to *prepare*. Throw it open to parents too, particularly if you're teaching lots of younger students.

I'm not going to go into any detail about what might be possible in such workshops—there are over 350 pages of practice techniques in *Practiceopedia* if you're stuck for suggestions—but the broad aim of the sessions would not be abstract theories of learning, but to cover the sorts of problems your students would be regularly confronting at home; from approaches to learning new pieces to speeding scales up; from triaging your practice todo list to getting your head ready for performance.

Whatever practice strategies you decide to focus on, these would be workshops with very different conversations from regular lessons: instead of the focus being on *what* students produce, it's on *how* they got there. Students will quickly realise that everyone wrestles with the same practice problems they do, and—most importantly—that there are many, many other ways of working apart from how they've worked so far.

The reward you promise for attending such sessions? That participants should end up being able to get more done in *less* time.

I'm obviously biased, but if I were to choose one club to be running regularly, it would very much be a practice skills workshop; the consequences for practicing going wrong are too dire for it not to be a priority for any studio that's serious about keeping students.

The **Static Studio** expects students to practice. The **Dynamic Studio** supports that expectation with in-depth help as to how to go about it.

Extension Option 6: Stagecraft and Performance

Traditional lessons are usually more about preparing students to *play* particular repertoire, rather than preparing students to *perform*—the two actually call on quite different skillsets. As we've all experienced when we watch our own students on recital day, it's entirely possible for the piece to be ready, but for the performance to fall flat...and, irritatingly, the very reverse, when otherwise underprepared students somehow *own* the stage on the big day, despite the fact that their lack of practice should have produced a train wreck.

Your Stagecraft and Performance Skills Club looks at how some students are able to command a stage like this; at how some performers are able to project icy calm, others radiant enthusiasm, while others simply seem terrified or bored. How can you use your piece's introduction to warm the audience and lift your confidence? Once onstage, under what circumstances should performers sit for a while and focus, and when alternatively should they simply bounce out and *launch*? How can they choose an appropriate tempo, when there's not a metronome in sight, and adrenaline is distorting their perceptions? What should they do if their accompanist chooses a tempo for them...and chooses badly? How can they gracefully rescue things if they get lost, or screw up an important passage? What can they do so that their bow looks gracious and engaging, rather than clunky and self-conscious? Under what circumstances would they take just one more curtain call, and when is it best to leave well enough alone?

Again, these sessions will look very different from regular lessons. Students would be practicing *starting* pieces, *ending* them, getting *to and from the stage*, no-fuss *tuning up*, judging *acoustics*, *communicating* with ensemble partners while playing, *controlling* tempos that are starting to run away, deciding whether to include or abandon *repeats*...

...all issues that they would eventually otherwise figure out for themselves after years of messing up—or you can fast track things for them with a series of classes that specifically gets them ready not just to *play*, but to sell a *performance*.

The **Static Studio** prepares *pieces*.
The **Dynamic Studio** prepares *performances*.

Extension Option 7: Music Technology Club

There's a chapter later in the book (➡253) where we'll take a closer look at some of the possibilities that technology can open for your studio, but *having* gear is nowhere near as exciting as what students will end up *doing with it*. One of the delicious realities of working with technology in the studio is that your students will quickly outstrip you: that prospect excites Dynamic studios as much as it terrifies teachers with a more Static outlook.

The phrase "the possibilities are endless" is overworked, but it's literally true of technology in the studio, because every day, new possibilities are being released.

So, for example, your music technology club might look at the **fundamentals of recording**, with the program focusing on the recording, editing and mastering of a Studio CD. Or it might serve as an **introduction to MIDI** composition. Or **virtual orchestration**, where students can hear for themselves what happens if they rescored the opening of the Rite Of Spring for cor anglais, or solo cello, instead of bassoon.

Alternatively, students could create **film scores**, or advertising jingles. Or you might explore the overlap between virtual instruments and sound effects, and run a unit on creating **sound-scapes.** Or students might **reverse engineer** and then recreate backing tracks to popular songs. Or record a **virtual octet**, despite the fact that the performers were never actually physically in the same space at the same time...and that there were actually only *three* performers...and that two of them were students emailing their contributions from *studios overseas...*

Students might **program their own synth sounds**, or produce tracks of Phillip Glass-like **minimalism**. They might use **notation software** like Sibelius or Finale to create their own arrangements, or repertoire for other students, or theory sheets.

There are more options outlined in that resourcing chapter, but what's particularly exciting is that you don't need a $100,000 recording studio to do all of this—all you need is a good computer and the right software. A Mac or a PC can easily become an entire symphony orchestra, or a big band, or a recording desk, or professional notation suite...or just about anything else that is used in music production.

What will your students produce? How much fun will they have in the process?

And how much more compelling is a studio that also offers all this over one that simply teaches you how to play your instrument?

The **Static Studio** doesn't have time for gadgetry, and wouldn't know how to use it in any case. The **Dynamic Studio** invests regularly in new technology, and learns how to make the most of it.

Extension Option 8: Aural Wizardry

Just as your studio extensions make it possible for students to *improvise pieces on the spot* (➡61), or *perform pieces they're seeing for the very first time* (➡63-175), you could run programs specifically to help students play just about anything *simply by hearing it.*

So again, this paves the way for a somewhat unusual and dramatic studio recital; instead of a student playing a piece they've been preparing for months, they'll perform something they—and the whole hall—heard for the first time just moments ago.

Again, the sort of interval training, melodic dictation, chord recognition and the like that would make up such a course is beyond the scope of this book, but whatever content you decide to focus on, the secret again is to ensure that everyone can succeed with whatever you *start* with, and then gradually ramp it up from there.

There's more at stake here than the play-anything-by-ear party trick: students who depend on dictation-type tests as part of their school music assessments will love the impact your help will have on their marks, while students who make use of recordings as part of learning new pieces (which should be everyone) will find that they're able to work out more than ever before without needing the cheat-sheet that is the score.

For your more competitive students, there's an additional compelling option: *aural training lends itself well to having students pit their skills against others.* Who can most correctly write out the Tough Atonal Melody Of The Week, after just four hearings? Or correctly identify the greatest number of these (increasingly tough) progressions? Or most accurately tap back these crazy polyrhythms after just *one* hearing? The results can be tabled, benchmarked, turned into awards, and highlighted in your Studio Newsletter: Aural training might well be intensive and thorough, but it doesn't have to be dull or lonely.

Most importantly though, *it gives students yet another way to shine:* you might have someone who struggles with reading and technical work, and hates the idea of performing in public, but who has always had a knack for being able to play by ear. Instead of struggling through traditional music lessons, they can become a superstar in your Aural Wizardry program.

The **Static Studio** expects all students to
read their way to instrumental proficiency.
The **Dynamic Studio** knows that there are
many, many other ways to achieve the same outcome.

Extension 9: HyperEnsembles

For most Static Studios, private music tuition means exactly that—one-on-one lessons, with a solo performance on concert day. The occasional novelty duet aside, each student is taught in their own little bubble, those bubbles kept separate and orderly by the weekly schedule gridlines.

As is so often the case, these constraints are not the result of lack of imagination—these same Static Studios will be well aware of the benefits of ensemble playing, but will have reasons for not implementing an ensemble program of their own. One of the common obstacles cited, for example, is that the studio *lacks requisite instrumentation*; the argument being that some instruments lend themselves more neatly to studio ensembles than others—that it's all well and good for a *singing* teacher to talk about ensembles, but it doesn't make so much sense if you exclusively teach *tuba*. Or *organ*. Or, for that matter, *piano*.

That's missing the point of what a studio ensemble is for though. You're not trying to win a Grammy, or conform to the expectations of a musicologist. You're simply trying to engineer opportunities for your students to play together. The fact that the ensembles might not be *balanced*, or have *native repertoire* is not going to matter to those taking part, or to the parents watching on recital day.

One of the most memorable performances I've ever heard consisted of a beaten-up upright piano on the steps of the Sydney Opera House, with an ensemble of four singers. The work they tackled? Carmina Burana. *All* of it. Ridiculous, with forces so small, and a thunky bar-room piano that was nowhere near in tune (you've never heard "O Fortuna" until you've heard it like *that*). But it quickly attracted a crowd, and set against the lights of Sydney Harbour, and a warm summer evening, it was just magical somehow. I've heard dozens of performances of this work, but this one, I remember.

The point wasn't the *ensemble*. It was the *fellowship*, and sheer joy of performance. Nobody who watched it came away unmoved.

What then might be possible in your own studio, once the constraints of *convention* or *precedence* are removed? What unexpected adventures could you unleash?

So, for example, how many pianists can you fit on one piano? (There was a hilarious video kicking around online of a concert in Denmark that featured 12 pianists playing the same piano). What arrangement could you come up with to have all 36 of your guitar students playing at the same time? Or perhaps instead 18 guitar duets? Or 12 trios? Or your best student as a soloist playing antiphonally with an ensemble consisting of everyone else?

> "...how much more fun will they have when it's not just music, but music with *other people?*"

Might it also be possible to set up *tiered* ensembles, to give students a series of promotions to aspire to? So students in the *beginner ensemble* would be hoping to be tapped on the shoulder to join the *intermediate* ensemble, who in turn want to be promoted to your *advanced* group, from whom the very best will be invited to constitute an *Elite Quartet*.

Or would you instead ignore student levels, and instead focus on where they live, so that students are *grouped by proximity of address*, and can therefore easily practice at each other's homes? Or maybe match students instead by *personality type?* Or have ensembles that are filled with students who love to play fast pieces, and some others that specialise in more lyrical works? Or deliberately partner *beginner* students with *advanced* students; an open-strings-only cello pedal point part for your six-year-old beginner grounding a virtuosic upper register showpiece from the most capable adult cellist in your studio?

When you start thinking about ensembles, the permutations and combinations are, well, as mathematically diverse as you'd expect from a sample that is large as your entire student body. That diversity represents *opportunity*, and some of the most memorable moments in your studio recitals.

Again, each of these options represents tickets to different futures for your studio. Once your ensemble program is in place, how different would sessions that are preparing students for these ensemble performances be from their regular weekly tutoring? How much more fun will they have when it's not just music, but music with *other people?*

I'm aware that I'm preaching to the converted for the most part here. The reason I included this in this list is just in case your studio doesn't have any sort of ensemble program up and running yet. No matter how hermit-like the instrument you teach might normally be, to condemn all your students to playing alone is a huge opportunity missed.

The **Static Studio** is content to work with each student *individually*, just like the schedule says. The **Dynamic Studio** engineers opportunities for students to *work together*, even if they have to bend reality and offend composers.

Extension 10: Mentorships

In the same way that ensembles get students *rehearsing* and *performing* together, mentorships give your students an opportunity to *teach* and *learn* together.

The idea is that those advanced students who want to take part in the program would be paired with a beginner for a semester, and given a piece that it's their responsibility to oversee. Beyond you being there to supervise the sessions, all decisions as to which issues in the piece should be a *priority*, what should be only *mentioned in passing* and what should be *ignored entirely* are up to that advanced student. How the beginner should be *practicing* the piece is up to the advanced student. Recommended solutions to *technical problems* will be up to the advanced student. Corrections in *posture, tone production, fingering, phrasing*...all up to the advanced student.

The performance that results will truly be a collaboration, between one of your newest and one of your longest standing pupils. The symbolism of this won't be lost on anyone.

And then in return, when your advanced student needs to dress-rehearse one of their own major works, their beginner student will be the first person in the studio apart from yourself to hear the piece. Maybe they'll give feedback; maybe they'll draw a picture or make up a story that matches what they heard. Either way, it helps reinforce the connection between the two students, while leaving the beginner student feeling special for having been invited to this advance screening.

This is an enormously useful exercise for everyone involved:

- The beginner gets to work closely with a person who is a living example of what many years of lessons with you produces. The message here? Stick around. Here's how good *you* could become too.

• Both students now have someone special to cheer on at the next studio recital. When the beginner is scanning the audience, they'll be looking for their *parents*, they'll be looking for *you*, and now they'll also be looking for their *mentor*. A very young student might even wave.

• The mentor knows that you hold them in high regard—there really is no better way to say "I trust you, and your musical judgement" than to make them responsible for another student you teach.

• This whole process is one of developing autonomy—the message to the student is it's *your* performance, *you* prepare it from beginning to end, *you* make the musical decisions—and is a tremendously important mind shift for the advanced student to make, particularly as they start to make their own transition to full independence.

• And perhaps most usefully of all, the mentor now has some basic teaching experience, having taken a student's piece from never-seen-it-before to ready-to-perform. (See the next section for where else this can head...)

Will the mentor or the beginner student leave the studio? It's entirely possible. Will they leave the studio *while the mentorship is active?* It's unlikely.

It wouldn't just be you they'd be letting down.

The **Static Studio** has the *teacher* as the ultimate and sole authority. The **Dynamic Studio** actively looks for ways that *students* can be helping—and thereby linked to— *each other.*

Extension 11: Teaching traineeships

Many advanced students will have the technical skills to be able to take students of their own, but would be much more confident, have more credibility, and do a much better job if they were able to find a training program that specifically prepared them for the adventure. If your studio were to offer such a program, then you've just created an entirely new reason for advanced students to stay—and for new advanced students to come aboard.

The traineeship has to be conducted without your other students feeling that their lessons are being compromised at all, so you'd need to secure permission from each student to have your Teacher Trainee sit in on, and occasionally run part of their lesson. The

> "...what does the fact that you're regarded as a *Teacher of Teachers* say about your own lessons?"

secret here is distribution: rather than scheduling your Trainee to the same student's lesson a dozen times (which really is disruptive), you're much better off—and your Trainee will see a wider spectrum of teaching—if they cover a dozen different students a few times each.

As well as creating opportunities for your Trainee to observe other lessons, it's also worth scheduling a regular session with them where talking about teaching is the only thing on the agenda. What did they take away from this week? Having seen Sally's meltdown when she was asked to play from memory, how should next lesson play out—should we follow up and push her again, or let it slide? What should practice instructions for Nicholas focus on? Why? Now that Piers has almost finished

Book 2, what do you think he should work on next? How can we get Erica more fired up about her lessons? How do we handle Lisa's mother, who is making lessons almost impossible with her constant interrupting? Why do you think Michael cried on Tuesday? How should we handle it if it happens again? How can we get Donna to work on her sightreading...without it being obvious to her that she's working on her sightreading?

These are all the sorts of questions that are constantly running through any music teacher's head, but knowing to ask them is the result of experience (for *experience* read: messing things up a lot). What you're offering your Trainee is an accelerated journey through and past much of this confusion, so that they're approaching their first year of teaching with the sort of lesson-smarts that would normally take a decade to acquire otherwise.

From traineeship to Certification

If your studio has been established long enough for your letter-head alone to inspire confidence, then you could even offer *certification*: those trainees that impressed you enough, and completed whatever additional criteria you laid out would have the right to include "Trained by..."on their advertisements. Not only does that give them a credibility advantage when they're otherwise starting out and unknown, but every time their teaching ad appears, the prestige of your own studio is enhanced.

Alternatively, if you live in a state with its own teacher certification system, your program could specifically prepare students to be able to meet those requirements.

Either way, make this program successful enough, and you might find students enrolling in your studio *just to take part in the Teacher Traineeship*. So be it. For some teachers, this might all evolve to a point where that's primarily what their teaching studio is about: training the trainers. Again, so be it. The whole point of this chapter is that there can be much more to running a teaching studio than teaching people how to play their instrument.

And from the point of view of your other students, what does the fact that you're regarded as a *Teacher of Teachers* say about your own lessons? Why would they go anywhere else when there is a Master Teacher right here?

The **Static Studio** *knows its place*, and would never see itself as a trainer of teachers. The **Dynamic Studio** *creates its place*, and ends up with a reputation that almost makes advertising unnecessary.

Extension 12: Expert Infusions

A Static Studio would never consider sharing the stage like this, but part of being a Dynamic Studio is having the self-confidence to invite other experts into the studio, as part of a series of workshops and special classes. The result is that you can *extend* your studio's offerings *beyond your own areas of expertise.*

This opens up a whole world of possibilities.

So, for example, there might be a celebrated accompanist in town who is sought after precisely because she is able to be performance ready on almost no notice, despite never having seen the piece before. What could your students learn about sightreading from this person? Or practicing under pressure? Or what's possible just from *looking* at a score? Or which keys you really need to be on top of to cover 95% of all repertoire? Or how to fudge gracefully and credibly, if the actual notes are just not going to be possible in time? Or how extract as much as possible from a single 30 minute rehearsal? Or how to rescue a performance when the person you're playing with has got themselves horribly, irretrievably lost?

All brilliantly useful insights, none of which most music teachers are as uniquely qualified to give as your special guest star was.

You might follow that a month later by having a composer run students through how they get from a sketch to a finished opus. Your visitor might also outline what tricks composers need to be aware of to make pieces *easier* or *more difficult*...and therefore, how to judge for yourself just how difficult a new work really is, just by looking at the score. They might also hear works by some of your composition students, and then leave the studio with a brand new work that one of your students will be premiering at the end of year recital.

One month after that, and you might get a choral conductor to talk through tricks they use to arrange works and bring performances to life, and how to think of your own pieces more as if they were being *sung* rather than just *played*.

Or a sitar player, talking about microtones and how their instrument has been traditionally taught; what might your lessons be like if you were to learn as they once did? Let's try it out for a week and see.

Or a person who *invents* musical instruments. A cross-pedalled 12 string hurdy-gurdy? An electric contrabassoon with MIDI autocorrection? Tell me you wouldn't be just a little bit curious to hear and see these gadgets in action...your students will be too.

None of these might be areas you know anything about. It doesn't matter; your students won't think less of you. On the contrary, it's your energy and enthusiasm that makes the ongoing Guest Expert program possible—it's just another of the many, many benefits of being in your studio, rather than the once-a-week-just-the-standard-music-lesson-only that your competitors provide.

The **Static Studio's** offerings *start and stop* with whatever the teacher knows how to do.
The **Dynamic Studio** offerings are as *wide* as its Guest Expert invitation list is *long*.

Extension 13: One piece, many ways

Students are forever being told that they should "make their interpretation their own", but quickly realise that the most certain way to be criticised in a lesson is not to conform to the score. For creative students in particular, this please-stick-to-what-the-composer-wants feels remarkably like paint-by-numbers, their role reduced to following instructions.

The aim of the One Piece, Many Ways Club is to not just accommodate, but *extend* such free-thinking students, and completely turns that teaching model on its head. All the students in the club would be working on exactly the same piece, but instead of their prime directive being to *honour the composer's intentions*, they're instead under instructions to ensure that *their interpretation doesn't even remotely sound like anybody else's*. To facilitate this, there's an interesting prohibition: the student who first proposes a particular approach to a passage gets Intellectual Property rights over that solution...nobody else is then allowed to use that idea for the same passage.

So if one student chooses to open the piece with an extended and gentle crescendo, then that's off-limits for everybody else. Other students could still do a *steep* crescendo, or a *double-dip* crescendo, or a *diminuendo*, or an *arch-shaped* rise and fall—or use an extended and gentle crescendo *somewhere else* in the piece—but the gradual crescendo at the opening has been set aside for the student who first proposed it.

With preferred interpretation options then being snapped up like players at an NBL draft, students who miss their first pick will be forced to find brand new ways to interpret the piece. Better still, they'll also hear plenty of workable alternatives to what they came up with, reinforcing the message that preparing a new piece can be a *creative act,* rather than simply *re-creative.*

For students who are frustrated by the just-do-as-you're-told approach of traditional teaching, this can mean the difference between continuing lessons and not.

Whatever the students end up coming up with, recital day promises to be unexpectedly interesting. Unexpected, because when the audience first sees that the same piece has been scheduled 12 times in a row, you'll be able to hear the groan; interesting because what they will actually hear is 12 *completely* different performances...and a compelling showcase of student imagination, and a great advertisement for your new club.

The **Static Studio** treats scores as instruction sheets, *to which* students must be *faithful*
The **Dynamic Studio** treats scores as a framework, *within which* students can *create.*

Extension Option 14: Extreme Scales Society

In most studios, technical work is dutifully suffered through like some sort of wholesome vegetable that nobody really likes. Of course, technical work *is* wholesome: the challenge is making it palatable.

Your Extreme Scales extension handles this by turning the whole thing into a competitive, challenge-based *sport*, where students try to outdo each other in a series of technical work trials that go way—and I mean an order of magnitude—beyond what students would be asked to do normally. Of course, to be ready for each challenge, students will need to train at home. (A more pejorative verb would be "practice", but let's not mention *that*.)

The key here is that most technical work has benchmarkable parameters, which means that, like the aural training solutions we looked at earlier (➡72), competition is easy enough to set up and calibrate. So, for example, technical work can be assessed for **reliability**—the student's ability to produce it *flawlessly on demand*, or *many times in a row*, or in a *high pressure situation*; it can be assessed for **raw tempo**, with students rewarded for being able to beat *personal bests*—or *other students*—or *benchmarked targets*; or **evenness of delivery**, where keyboard players in particular can record their scale into a program like Logic or Cubase, and then be able to clearly see how many notes were *behind*, *ahead* or *dead on the beat*, and exactly *how loud* each note was relative to the others; or **versatility**, where students might need to deliver technical work using *challenging rhythms*, or confusing *dynamic schemes*, or with their *eyes closed*, or *two different scales at once*, or with *inconveniently placed accents* (1st, 4th, 11th and 17th notes please), or...

...there are *so* many possibilities, and even otherwise recalcitrant students will find that it's actually a lot of fun to rack up these various Achievements.

Again, at the recital, you can showcase this—it's a great stage for the Finals for some of your various events. And with all the cheering and fist pumping and sportcaster-style hypeups and announcements and trophies, you've done something that's never happened with scales and arpeggios before...

...you've made them *exciting*.

(If you're a piano teacher stuck for ideas on just how insanely tough—and fun—technical work challenges can be, *Scales Bootcamp* at InsideMusicTeaching.com lists over 3,000 scales -based Achievements to earn(!), ranging from insultingly easy to brain-and-finger-crunchingly bewildering.)

The **Static Studio** makes scales and other such technical work *compulsory*. The **Dynamic Studio** makes scales and other such technical work *compelling*.

Other possibilities:

Once you embrace the idea of extensions to your studio offerings, the possibilities are not only limitless, but there's no reason that your offerings *this* year have to be the same as what's available to students *next* year. This means that you can trial an extension, and if it doesn't work, quietly ditch it, and move on to something else.

So what else is possible, beyond those we've already looked at? Where to start...

You could offer **in-depth theory training**—not the half-dozen-questions-on-a-sheet that are usually shoehorned into your regular lessons, but classes that go way, way beyond the requirements of anything students will encounter at school or for theory exams. Part of the aim would be to ensure that anybody who does music lessons with you is going to get stellar grades if they also do music at school.

You might offer classes in **composition**, with students learning to arrange pieces, compose for each other, or using your virtual symphony orchestra—I'll put some examples of such orchestras from different software developers up at insidemusic-teaching.com so you can hear what I mean) (You won't believe what's possible now just using a Mac or PC)

You might set up a club that regularly **attends**, and then **reviews concerts**. So the next time there's the finals of an international violin competition or a celebrated jazz quintet in your city, Seats 12-31 in Row N might be filled with your students. You'd meet in the following week to talk about what you'd heard, students might then post their own reviews to your studio website. That same group might also be responsible for writing short reviews of every performance in your next recital—a compilation of which is a wonderful resource and memento for performing students to be able to take away.

An alternative to this is to have a review group that meets, and each week **assesses submitted recordings** from other students in your studio. The students featured on those recordings then end up with a dozen or more different written perspectives on their performance, while their own absence from the feedback process makes it more likely that the responses will be honest. The result? Plenty to think about for that student, and a honing of assessment skills for those in the group itself.

Another possibility is to run a series of **Zero-Help Workshops**, where students attending perform works that they've learned from scratch with no input from you whatsoever—the expectation is not that such performances would be just as good as if your help had been available (that would *not* be a good advertisement for continuing lessons), but to provide powerful evidence to students and parents alike that the lessons are heading in the right direction. After all, just *listen* to what your child is now able to produce all by themselves...

Closely related to this are **Peer Mediated Workshops**, where students perform for each other, and give all feedback, much as they would for any performance workshop, but your role here would not be as facilitator, but simply a fly on the wall. So if a solution for the uninspired opening for a particular performance is to be found, the suggestions will need to come from your students: no matter how much you might be itching to contribute your brilliant idea, this is not the forum. Again, it's about more steps towards student independence; surely the ultimate goal of every teacher.

Or you might step sideways from performance and feedback related activities, and run a regular course on **instrument maintenance**...or, if you have the skills (or contacts) actually **building** instruments. How should students choose reeds? Or strings? What is a sure sign that a piano needs voicing? Is it possible to teach your students to actually *tune* a piano? (Not to be confused with teaching your students to be a *piano tuner*—there's a reason that takes years of training—but all pianists should know how to quickly fix a faulty unison, for example) And if you're worried that such a class couldn't be sustained as a weekly event, then remember: *it's your studio.* You might run your instrument maintenance class just twice a year, as an option for those who are interested...

...along with all the other things that you're running twice a year, or fortnightly, or on the First Wednesday in Every Month, or just-during-winter, or as a once-only opportunity. Music lessons are still very much at the core of what you do, but there's much, much more on offer—parents describing your studio to others will scarcely know where to begin.

And Static Studios will look positively anaemic by comparison.

Putting it all together: the studio recital

This is where the time and effort you've spent on these extensions can really help your studio shine. The fact that your studio is offering a lot more than just how-to-play-your-instrument opens the way for a recital unlike any other students and parents have experienced before.

Sure, they'll hear *performances of pieces*, just like they would in any other teaching studio, although in there somewhere will be the beginner playing the piece that her mentor coached. And there will also be *ensembles*, large and small, traditional and unlikely. Nothing too out of the ordinary so far.

But thanks to the diverse offerings of your studio, they'll also hear a segment featuring students *making up a piece on the spot* (thanks to your Whose Note Is It Anyway Workshops), another with students performing a piece that they've *never seen before* (members of your Hardcore Sightreading Club), and yet another with students playing a piece that they—and the whole room— have only *heard for the first time moments ago*, and have no music for (the best and brightest from your Aural Wizards).

This same audience might also have watched a demonstration from students in your Extreme Scales Society complete with stopwatches, commentary and fist-pumping. They might have seen another segment in which one student played the same short piece 5 times in a row in *5 completely different ways*, showcasing the work that goes on in your One Piece, Many Ways club. Or another segment featuring works *composed* by students in the studio. Or another featuring beginners who were prepared by senior students in your Teaching Trainee program. Or the world premiere of the work composed by your Guest Star composer, who workshopped all your students earlier in the year. Or another by students who were inspired by your visiting musical instrument inventor, with performances on instruments they've made themselves. Or the segment of your concert featuring nothing but film music adaptations, because that was the theme for your Stylemasters club this semester. Or another featuring the launch of a Studio CD; recorded, edited, and the cover designed and photoshopped entirely by your Music IT students...

...ok, so somewhere we've crossed the fine line between a studio recital and Cirque du Soleil, but in a world where studio recital normally means an endless procession of students playing The Piece They've Been Working On, even to throw in *one* of these unexpected elements is going to send home parents and students amazed. And for students of the internet age, make no mistake: *amazed* is a very good state for them to go home in.

So I return to the question that started this chapter: what is there for students in your studio to *do?*

Is vanilla really the only ice-cream flavour you've got?

The **Static Studio** recognises vanilla as a *classic*; it was good enough for their teacher, and their teacher's teacher. The **Dynamic Studio** would have vanilla as *one of many flavours*, and ice cream as just *one of many treats*.

What's next:

Diversification can give students many additional reasons to stay in your studio, but it will all still quickly count for nothing if the lessons themselves fail a basic *convenience* test. Parents in particular can be unimpressed by even the best intentions if it makes their delicately balanced week unmanageable.

In the spotlight in the next chapter is something that is a constant source of frustration, causes tens of thousands of students to quit lessons every day, but is rarely talked about...

...this is probably the first book on music teaching to devote an entire chapter to the surprisingly fertile topic of *scheduling*.

Dynamic Scheduling

Escaping the grid

Dynamic Scheduling

THERE ARE FEW CLEARER INDICATORS OF a Static Studio than when a teacher refers to "my" teaching schedule. In doing so, they're claiming ownership over something that doesn't belong to them at all: teachers don't schedule on behalf of a *studio*, they schedule on behalf of *individual students that comprise that studio*, people for whom it is much more inconvenient to attend their scheduled lesson, than it is for the teacher to host it.

> "...you'll be amazed just how many lesson times you'll be able to *upgrade*. Think airlines and seats; it means lots of happier families."

In short, these times don't belong to the teacher; they belong to the student.

It's a subtle distinction, but, as we'll see, there's nothing subtle about the student retention disasters that getting this wrong can unleash.

Of course, when such Static schedules are printed out, they do present as being the very model of organisation and efficiency: see how all the Monday students are lined up under "Monday!"; behold, all the 4pm students aligned across the page, right there, next to the 4! Such order!

It might be *order*, but it's not *planning*. Hidden beneath the tidy exterior is the unruly history of how it came to be—most music teachers' schedules fill up with all the unregulated first-in-best-dressed space-grab of a shopping mall car park on sale day.

None of this matters until the schedule is starting to be full, but at that point the true price for ad-hoc scheduling will become horribly clear: *the tightly wedged clutter that is the teaching week can make it very difficult to accommodate changes.* Finding more convenient times for parents becomes too difficult to seriously consider in anything short of an emergency, which is why we don't…as long as there are no active complaints, we'll keep the lesson time exactly as it is, sometimes for years.

But remember, the most dangerous levels of dissatisfaction— the kind that has students "taking a break"—don't always come with active complaints. Whether they're protesting or not, a student who is stuck with a lesson time that's even moderately inconvenient is a student you're much more likely to lose; if you've allowed your studio schedule to simply *evolve*, rather than periodically *engineering* it, then you may well have a dozen such student time bombs right now.

> "...an ill-considered and unsupervised schedule is a silly, silly reason to lose a student, but it is sufficient."

An ill-considered and unsupervised schedule is a silly, silly reason to lose a student, but it is sufficient, particularly in an age when students and parents accommodate their desire to do *everything* by overcommitting.

But how can something as grid-rigid and orderly as scheduling be subject to Dynamic Studio thinking? Surely if any aspect of teaching has to be fixed and predictable, it's this?

Not so. It turns out that scheduling doesn't have to be fixed *or* predictable, and works best with a constantly *evolving* structure that will only vaguely resemble the sort of timetable you've been using all these years.

Let's take a look at how it works; the whole process actually starts with literally nothing at all.

Clearing the decks

The traditional Static Studio scheduling logjam all stems from the wrong question being asked when the teacher is first allocating a lesson time. What normally happens is that the teacher looks at their schedule, finds a gap, and then asks something like "Hey, how about Thursdays at 5?".

That sheds some light on whether Thursdays at 5 works. But it's a closed question: the answer reducible to a "yes" or "no", neither of which gives any usable information about the dozens of *other* timeslots that make up your teaching week.

Worse still, when the Static Studio schedules via questions like this, it does so one student at a time, one timeslot at a time, and only when it absolutely needs to.

By contrast, a Dynamic approach to scheduling begins with an entirely different question; one that's designed to prompt *open-ended* answers, is asked of *everyone*—whether already scheduled or not—and is asked *regularly*:

> "Here is a list of **all the times that this studio runs lessons**. Could you please rate each time on the following scale":
>
> ☠ impossible
>
> ☹ doable but painful
>
> ☺ neutral
>
> ☺ works well for us
>
> ☑ works brilliantly for us

This doesn't just give the teacher information about one student, for one lesson time, for a contingency that has just arisen. This is a comprehensive survey of *every student* and *every possible lesson time* so that you're ready for *whatever might arise.*

Armed with that information, the teacher can then create a schedule from scratch that doesn't just make lessons possible, but has been actively designed to accommodate each student's preferences.

I say "create from scratch", because the only way to get this done is to completely clear your schedule, and start over. It's a little like trying to figure out how to get that last suitcase into your car's trunk; if it already seems overfull, it's almost always easier to take everything out, and start again.

And if circumstances change, and a student suddenly needs to find a new lesson time, the system means you don't have to make dozens of phone calls to find out what sort of swap might work. You *know* what works, because you've got confirmation of all the

> "...the humble teaching schedule is actually a much more powerful tool for engineering change than most teachers suspect."

"works well for us" and "works brilliantly for us" times from all your students, right there in front of you. So when you're doing the inevitable *A goes to B's time who goes to C who bumps to A*, you can keep A, B and C as happy as possible; you'll also quickly be able to see which students should be A, B and C in the first place.

The result won't be perfect—it's very unlikely that you'll be able to put everyone in their "Works brilliantly for us" timeslots— but you'll be amazed just how many students whose lesson time you were able to *upgrade*. Think airlines and seats; it means lots of happier families.

As long as you regularly put out these lesson time surveys, so that your snapshot of parents' preferences is always as current as possible, this is a simple Dynamic Studio technique that will

revolutionise your ability to give students great lesson times…
and decrease the chances of them deciding they don't need a
lesson time after all.

The Static Studio takes bookings in the order
received, makes changes only when necessary,
and expects students to accommodate.
The Dynamic Studio hits "reset" regularly, and
asks everyone yet again: *what suits you best?*

Using all the numbers on the clock

If the first principle underpinning a Dynamic schedule is to
periodically erase everything and start over, the second is to look
at what might be possible if entire schedule segments can *slide*.

Most teaching studios seem to run schedules that either
align neatly to the top of the hour, or exactly halfway between:
3:00, 3:30, 4:00, and so on. Timetabling lessons that way might
be *tidy*, it might be *traditional*, but insisting that lessons should
start just because the big hand is on the six or the twelve is ultimately arbitrary; it fails to take into account the limitations and
opportunities that your students' own schedules present.

One such consideration is whatever schedule your local school
happens to run to. If you're planning on offering lessons that are
"straight after school", then it's madness to create those lesson times
until you understand what "straight after school" actually means.

What time does the bell ring? What time do students
actually then get out? How long is the drive/walk to your studio?

Answer those three questions, add 10 minutes as a buffer, and
you know the start time for your first lessons of the afternoon. It's

nothing to do with *tidy* or *but-lessons-are-always-on-the-hour*, instead it's based directly on reality. Which means that if these calculations suggest a 3:40 lesson time instead of 3:30, then you should listen and make it so; to do otherwise is to either set up students to be **late** (if you opt for 3:30), or to put off your first lessons until 4pm, and have 20 minutes of **dead time** during what should be prime teaching time...

...in which case—multiplied by the 5 days of the school week—you've actually lost 100 minutes in prime time...*enough to have scheduled an additional three students(!)*

The second advantage to offset times like this is the flow-through effect it has on the rest of your teaching schedule: in this example your entire afternoon will then presumably be offset by 10 minutes—3:40, 4:10, 4:40, 5:10 etc. Given that most of the other commitments parents need to juggle will start or end at :00 and :30 times, *your times now no longer collide directly with those commitments.* Parents don't have to be in two places at once any more—you've given them a 10 minute window to get to you, and a 20 minute window after the lesson to then get where they need to be next (think about it...)

This technique is another example of not just automatically doing something in a particular way just because that's the way it's always been done. It's your studio. You get to make up the rules. They might as well make life easier for everyone.

The **Static Studio** starts lessons on the hour, and at half past the hour, just like everyone else. The **Dynamic Studio** is not nearly so superstitious, and prefers *expedient* times to *tidy* ones. (when was the last time a NASA rocket launched at exactly 4pm?)

Taking into account what comes *before* and *after*...

So far we've *reset* lesson times, and *slid* them; the next consideration is how they might most usefully be *sequenced*. This means instead of simply scheduling each student in isolation, you'd also be factoring in who follows and precedes each student.

It's not always possible, but much of this process will revolve around ensuring students who are linked *outside* the studio are offered contiguous lessons *inside* the studio.

Willingness to create related back-to-back lesson times like this means that parents of **sibling students** only have a single trip to and from lessons each week to organise, while students whose lesson times are paired (or trebled!) because they're **friends** will be able to carpool, and then potentially work together during their lessons.

The latter in particular is a significant gain for the retention-aware Dynamic Studio: your music lessons then become yet another thing those friends have in common, making the decision to stop lessons that much more complicated for both of them. As was the case with mentoring (➡77), the decision to leave affects more people than just student and teacher.

This all might seem like common sense, but many Static Studios have policies in place that actively ensure siblings and friends are *not* timetabled back-to-back, lest there be Comparisons or Other Unpleasantries. But even when this is a valid concern, there are other ways to achieve the separation needed without doubling the number of trips to your studio that parents need to plan their week around.

You could, for example, set up a waiting room that's out of earshot. Or simply give the waiting sibling some headphones, an old iPad, and tell them that no student has been able to complete all 10 of these *Angry Birds* levels in one lesson. Or set up the waiting chair so that it faces *away* from the lesson, with a set of headphones, recordings and scores on hand so they can preview upcoming repertoire (➡168). Or a book of origami, a stack of paper, and a challenge to make as many of the showcased models as they can before the lesson ends. Or an ongoing story that every waiting student has to contribute to (➡218). It really doesn't matter what the distraction is—it's very, very easy to get one student so engaged in what they're doing that they don't notice the other student. In doing this, you're also ensuring that they don't mind the wait—in fact, sometimes the student can be faintly disappointed when it's time for their lesson to actually start. (That's fine!)

For most pairs of students though this sort of enforced separation is an opportunity lost; there are rich lesson possibilities when there is a second student in the room which transcend any concerns about unpleasant comparisons. This is someone who can *give feedback*, or be a *duet partner*, or call out *which scales will be tested today*, or *turn pages*, or *hold the video camera* to capture the performance, or *circle the dynamics* the other student missed, or *provide a steady beat* for the other student to stay with, or *deliberately attempt to distract* the other student while they're running a concentrate-no-matter-what dress rehearsal, or *conduct* the other student's performance, or *create the theory questions* that will be the other student's homework, or *use a highlighter* to mark the parts of the piece that were talked about most during the lesson, or *help create practice instructions* for the week ahead...

...it's not a group lesson, or a competition, but it is a shared experience. And best of all, the student *watching and helping* will be learning just as much as the student who's actually playing.

Tactical pairings

Not all engineered pairings need to be between students who are related or friends; sometimes the pairings can be entirely tactical.

So, for example, you might deliberately timetable a *talented-but-unmotivated* intermediate student to have their lesson immediately after the most *outstanding and switched on* advanced student in the studio. Or engineer a reunion by scheduling an older student straight after that younger student that they *used to mentor* a couple of years ago (➥77). Or a student who is starting scales, but can't see the point, straight after a student who is a member of your Extreme Scales Society (➥85), *loves* working with scales, and can blast through the various scales games that you're then able to run.

Or a pair of students who are *already working on a duet*, just before another student who you are hoping will *want to work on a duet*...who in turn has their lesson just before the person who you are hoping *will become their duet partner.*

Such manipulations! And much of the time, the students will have no idea what you're up to. Mwuhahaha!

Possibilities in a Dynamic Studio are endless, but most of them are easier to implement if they can be *seeded*—a teaching schedule can gently nudge students to wanting exactly what you need them to, and is therefore not just a tool for *convenience*, but an agent for *change*.

For the **Static Studio** the question
of whose lesson is before
or after whose is entirely arbitrary.
For the **Dynamic Studio,** it's a chess move.

Rethinking weekly lessons

Music studios everywhere seem to teach students once a week, but while the weekly contact definitely has advantages, there's no rule that says this is how your studio needs to run. A big cost for families committing to music lessons is the impact it has on their own own schedules; a weekly lesson means that stress hits once a week, every week, guaranteed.

One easy way to literally halve this time-stress for parents is to dispense with tradition and offer *fortnightly* lessons, with those lessons running twice as long as weekly lessons normally would. The doubling of the lesson length ensures that students get the same number of contact hours with you in each semester, but otherwise offers benefits many time-poor families will find helpful:

> "...with two full weeks between lessons, students will have twice the time to prepare..."

• They'd get every second week "off", creating a little space in their otherwise crazy schedules.

• The fact that the lesson is an hour long gives parents time to drop-and-run, with 50 minutes to get grocery shopping done, or take a sibling to ballet, or whatever, rather than the (uselessly short) window that a traditional lesson offers.

• With two full weeks between lessons, students will have twice the time to prepare—this means that if they lose a few days to a school camp/being sick they haven't lost an entire lesson preparation campaign in the process, which means fewer missed lessons.

Not all parents will be interested in fortnightly lessons. But as a Dynamic Studio, you wouldn't be making this *compulsory* across your entire studio; it would simply be an *option* for those families that could use the breathing space. You'll almost certainly be the only studio in town to be so accommodating.

The Static Studio only offers weekly lessons, because that's just what's *done*. **The Dynamic Studio** prefers to think laterally about its scheduling options to better accommodate time-pressed families.

Rethinking scheduled lessons

Extrapolate the logic underpinning fortnightly lessons far enough, and you eventually end up with an intriguing possibility: what if some students were to have no scheduled lessons whatsoever?

> "Just imagine: lessons happening when they're *needed*, rather than when they simply *fall due*"

It's a complete rethink of the traditional lesson model: instead of the student turning up to *regular appointments*, they would instead *request* lessons as they need them. So in the leadup to a big scholarship audition, you might end up seeing them several times in one week. But when the time comes for them to become familiar with a major concerto, they might go for two months before they felt that it was ready for your input, rather than wasting your time while they're learning all the notes.

This lessons-on-demand model is similar to how postgraduate students might work with a supervisor, and is best suited to students who sometimes need a month or two to pull things together, and are able to work well without supervision. That's definitely not everyone. But it will probably be *someone*, if you're open to the possibility.

It's actually a scheduling method I've used many times for advanced students, and I highly recommend it—apart from helping ensure that there are no "dead" lessons, it also frees up a slot on your regular schedule. You can either charge students for every lesson they actually have, or have what is effectively a flat membership fee for the studio, with up to X lessons included as part of that.

Just imagine: lessons happening when they're *needed*, rather than when they simply *fall due*...teaching ends up being very, very different.

The **Static Studio** sees every student
every week, *ready or not.*
The **Dynamic Studio** sees some students
only when those students *request the help*

Rethinking Studio Lessons

There is one scheduling possibility that offers students even more convenient than the lessons-on-demand model, although many teachers find the very thought blasphemous:

What if your students were to have the option at any time not to have to come to your studio *at all*, but to run the lesson instead via Skype or Facetime?

Now before you tut-tut and skip ahead to the next idea, just think through what this option would mean. There would be no travelling, no need for parents to pick anybody up—short of actually doing house calls (which is almost always a colossally inefficient way to run a studio, and an idea you won't see in this book anywhere) this is the most convenient you can make things for the people you teach. You'd be in your studio, your student would be, well, wherever really.

> "Instead of students texting just before a lesson to say
>
> *"running late, sorry"*,
>
> they might send
>
> *"Running late: could we skype today instead?"* "

A lot of teachers would never consider this, citing the fact that it's just not the same as having the student there in front of you. They're missing the point entirely, but they also happen to be right: it's *not* the same.

You can't, for example, physically correct a student's bow hold or write on their score. But you can still give feedback as to whether their chosen tempo is appropriate, or sustainable, or consistent. You can still interrupt to remind them that that F sharp is *still* supposed to be a sharp at the very end of the measure. And that those staccatos would work better if they were even crisper.

You can still give practice instructions, and check that troublesome rhythm on page 2. And if it remains troublesome, you can demonstrate what the correct rhythm is. You can still assess sightreading, hear scales, ask to hear that bit one more time please, clap to keep them in time while they play, talk up (or down) dynamics while they play...

...in short, while there are things you can't do, the list of what you *can* do is long, varied and significant enough for you to be able to run viable lessons.

Remember the proposal here is not to teach this way exclusively—or even regularly—but for it to be an *option*. For a family whose car is in being repaired, or who has a parent overseas, or a student with a broken leg, or who is interstate for two months...or for that matter, a young student who just loves the whole lessons-on-my-computer atmosphere...your willingness to consider the unthinkable will be appreciated.

It means that instead of students texting you just before a lessons to say "running late, sorry", they might send "Running late: could we skype today instead?"

Say *no*, and you get a traditional lesson, but perhaps only 15 minutes, working with a stressed and breathless student. Say *yes*, and you're limited to whatever is possible via a video lesson, but you will get the full half-hour, and a student who's grateful because you've just rescued them from being late...to say nothing of parents who now no longer have to leave the house at all.

No matter how you think you feel about video lessons, you should at least try a couple before you make up your mind. It's a studio-changing option to have on standby.

The **Static Studio** *rejects* video lessons outright because of the medium's *limitations*.
The Dynamic Studio *embraces* video lessons because of the medium's *opportunities*.

Treating punctuality dynamically...

When I was a postgraduate student, there was a lecturer who would famously lock the lecture theatre as the clock ticked over to the scheduled start time—no matter how much late students might pound on the doors and protest, they were simply marked absent, and the lecture would proceed without them.

That might seem like tough love, but there are plenty of studio music teachers who have similar policies on punctuality, differing from this extreme only by degree. As a late student, you might not be *locked out,* but you'll be *lectured* or *made to wait even longer* or *issued with the first of Three Strikes And You're Out* or *(inset your preferred retribution here).*

> "Remember, the phrase you don't ever want parents using about your lessons is "it's all too hard" "

The problem with a policy like that is that you don't just catch those students who are casual with punctuality. This is driftnet fishing; you're going to catch all sorts of students that the policy was never designed to punish.

So you'll catch students who legitimately get caught in traffic. Or students who were otherwise reluctant to come to the lesson, and talked into it in your studio's driveway. (Only to be hit with a *lecture* when they do finally come in…what were you *thinking?*…). Or students who were only late because Dad is always late picking them up. Or students who were late because the car that dropped them was coming straight from a little sister's basketball game that ran overtime. Or any number of other contingencies that make the ideal of punctuality just that—an ideal, not always compatible with the slings and arrows of, well, reality of any sort.

Remember, *the greater the stress your lessons cause, the more dispensable those lessons become.* I'm not advocating that a Dynamic Studio appease serial latecomers; I'm saying that while a blanket and unforgiving punctuation policy might lead to more 30 minute rather than 25 minute lessons, it does so by dialling up the blood pressure of every parent in your studio. Static studios cause stress because *the teacher's* refusal to bend means *parents* have to.

This is particularly true of today's insanely busy students, who were probably coming *from* something else, and then on their way *to* somewhere else at lesson's end.

Dynamic punctuality sounds like an oxymoron, but it's just a reminder that a Dynamic Studio is no place to get all Mussolini on your students about punctuality—except for, as we'll see in the next section—the time lessons are supposed to *end*.

The **Static Studio** has *clear and unwavering expectations* regarding punctuality. The **Dynamic Studio** understands that punctuality is important, but that sometimes, *stuff happens.*

...but making sure you end on time.

Being a Dynamic Studio isn't just about imagining what you *could* do; it's also very much about being clear on what you *shouldn't* do. Most Dynamic Studios would love, for example, to be able to continue lessons past the allotted end time—having to stop just because the clock says so is a frustrating reason to interrupt things when you're on a roll.

However, to do so would actually make the classic Static Studio mistake of only seeing the world through the studio's eyes. For parents, lessons will often have been shoehorned in between other activities that are on the same day, and scheduled at almost the same time—the result is a sequencing sheet that has the parent feeling like an air-traffic-controller at LAX: *drop Sally off* at math tutoring; *pick up Angus* from Alex's house; *drop Angus* at his music lesson; when the lesson ends, go *pick up Sally* from math tutoring, then try to *catch the second half* of Denise's basketball match...

If just one of those events runs late, the result is a cascade that flows right through the rest of the afternoon, and then *everything* is late. As a parent of three kids, I know how stressful that can be, and I don't think good thoughts about whoever it was that tipped the first domino.

One all-too-common stress inducing scenario is when the Static Studio—which reserves the right to extend lessons as need be (check the studio policy, it's right there)—takes it upon itself to have the outgoing student play a "quick" duet with the incoming student, *with the parent sitting in the car in the driveway,* who has no idea what's going on. The absence of communication cuts both ways: the teacher has got no way of being able to see what sort of stress this extra 5-10 minutes might be causing; the parent has no way of knowing when their child is going to appear, or why they're running late.

That parent won't necessarily be sounding their horn when the 5:30 lesson is still not over by 5:42...but if they've got another child to pick up by 5:45, then they're probably using language about their child's music teacher that I won't print in a family-friendly book like this.

Remember, the phrase you don't ever want parents using about your lessons is "it's all too hard". Fall into that category, and it doesn't matter how excellent your teaching is: you will lose that student.

The key distinction here between the Static Studio and the Dynamic Studio is not the *creative drive* to want to do things like extend lessons—Static Studios are often run by highly creative teachers—it's the willingness to *collaborate* in engineering solutions, rather than simply *announcing* them. If The Dynamic studio is considering running overtime, it would take the parent's temperature first—ideally, with those parents actually sitting right there in the studio, so you can sense when goodwill starts to be replaced with *ok, it's enough already now.*

> "...just because there was no charge for that extra 10 minutes doesn't mean there was no *cost...*"

It's something that Static Studios overlook to their peril, but just because there's no *charge* for an extra 10 minutes here or there doesn't mean that there was no *cost*—your "generosity" is not so helpful if it means the student's big brother ends up being benched at his basketball match because he missed the start.

The **Static Studio** extends lessons as the need arises.
The **Dynamic Studio** has end times families can safely plan the rest of their afternoon around.

And finally, whatever the lesson time, make it a sanctuary...

For those parents who sit in each week, your music lessons are just one of many instances where they're captive spectators—think soccer matches, speech nights, debates, school plays, information evenings, exhibitions...trapped-in-a-chair is a routine and inescapable part of having kids.

This wouldn't be so bad if the time spent could be more engaging; the problem is that as teachers, we have a skewed perspective of just how interesting that half hour is. The 30 minutes of a music lesson will go by quickly enough for both teacher and student, because they're main characters in the play, but for the parent—usually in a chair with little to occupy them otherwise—the same 30 minutes can feel interminable.

If you're a teacher worried about losing students, that sort of ennui on the part of fee-paying parents spells danger.

So what can be done?

> "...like any good host, you're anticipating the needs of your guests...make them feel welcome and they'll want to stay."

The final Dynamic Studio scheduling challenge is to transform that waiting experience into something parents actually look forward to; a thirty minute oasis of calm and comfort that contrasts with the rest of their crazy week.

It all starts with an experiment where you put yourself in their shoes:

Next time you have an afternoon free, *spend half an hour sitting wherever it is that you expect parents to sit while they wait for lessons.* Don't cheat on the time: make sure you're there for every second of the thirty minutes.

You'll get a first hand and disturbingly honest perspective of what it really means for parents to have to sit in on each lesson; of what they're giving up each week, apart from the lesson fees and their time.

As a Dynamic Studio, you're able to change all, most, some or none of what you're expecting parents to put up with. Let's take a look at what you should be checking for:

Assessing what you expect them to sit in

Forget about whether the fabric matches the curtains, and whether that small hole in the armrest should be repaired; you have to stop thinking like an interior decorator, and instead like a parent who needs to pass 30 minutes. So:

How easy is it to *read a book* in this chair? Or *use a laptop?* Or read a *newspaper?* Or have a *nap?* How well will it accommodate *larger parents?* Is it possible to *put your feet up?* Is there somewhere for them to rest a *soft drink or coffee?*

No matter how convenient the lesson time, if you've got parents spectating from a ramrod-backed hardwood church-pew-discard that you bought at an Amish garage sale, you're creating half an hour that even the biggest fan of your work will dread. Remember, it's not just about comfort, it's about parents being able to spend the time in their preferred way; with music lessons representing around 20 hours every year spent in whatever chair you provide, this small detail is actually a key factor in whether they *look forward* to lessons, or *dutifully suffer* through them. Every parent has a tolerance for the latter, but the suffering is both real, and noted.

My recommendation? Parents should not only be sitting in the most comfortable, usable chair you own, but something that's more welcoming than anything they're likely to sit in at home. It might seem like a trivial asset, but ask yourself—if one of the events at which you were a regular captive spectator meant that you had to spend time in the most comfortable chair you'd ever sat in, *and then had half an hour where the world was making no demands of you whatsoever*, wouldn't you be looking forward to it just a little bit?

It's not going to rescue lessons if the student's problem is that they can't decide if they hate you or their instrument more, but when there's vacillation from a family who is perhaps otherwise dangerously neutral towards lessons (and *neutral* is always *dangerous*) it can help ensure that the scales don't tip.

The **Static Studio** makes sure that waiting parents have something to *sit on*. The **Dynamic Studio** makes sure waiting parents have something comfortable to *relax in*.

Anticipating their needs

OK, so the chair itself is a joy to spend time in. The pampering doesn't end there though: again, picture yourself stuck in the lesson as a spectator for 30 minutes. Could you get yourself a drink of water? Or a snack? Or a coffee? Can you read today's paper? What other reading material is to hand? How varied, current and interesting is it? Does your studio have wifi for their tablet, phone or laptop? Does using the toilet mean interrupting the lesson to get a map of the house, or is its location clearly marked, and permission to use it whenever pregranted?

Like any good host, you're anticipating the needs of your guest and making sure everything is to hand—make them feel welcome, and they'll want to stay.

Operators of indoor kid's adventure playgrounds are all too well aware of this principle; most of them have lounges to sit in, newspapers and magazines to read, coffee to drink, air-conditioning to relax in, all designed to make the time spent at the facility something that the parent looks forward to as much as their child does. (It works on me…I'm very, very happy to take my 6 year old to places like this; he gets to rampage on the equipment, I get to have a coffee and read, and all the while I'm earning My Dad Is So Cool Because He Takes Me To Fun Places points.)

> "…if you had half an hour where the world was making no demands of you whatsoever, wouldn't you be looking forward to it just a little bit?"

The **Static Studio** equips their studio so the *teacher* has everything they need. The **Dynamic Studio** equips their studio so that students *and parents* have everything they need.

Neutralising any environmental quirks

As well as auditing the *resources* of the waiting area, it's also important to be aware of—and then address—any *environmental oddities* that might compromise the oasis of calm that you're trying to set up for the parents who sit in on lessons, and pay the bills. Again, the only way you can honestly check for these issues is to actually spend time in the chair:

Do afternoon sunbeams shine in their eyes, or make this part of the room uncomfortably hot? Or does proximity to that window that you like to keep open mean that you teach lessons with a wind-chill factor?

If they arrive 10 minutes early, is there anywhere for parent and student to sit, or do they need to stand until the previous student (and their parent) are gone? And when it is their child's turn, does the parent have to get up to let people squeeze past every time someone comes into the room?

When they're seated, does the orientation of the room or a badly positioned bookshelf make it impossible for them to clearly see their child during the lesson? And is that bookshelf full of professional development books and music titles that add to the credibility and energy of your studio? Or are there titles—professional or otherwise—there that you'd rather they didn't see? (Is your daughter reading *Mein Kampf* for her Fall History class, and leaving it next to your copy of *Norton's Anthology of Western Music?*)

Does clutter mean that it's difficult for tall parents to stretch out their legs, so that the whole lesson feels like half an hour in a domestic economy class airline seat? Is their space well lit to be able to comfortably read in evening lessons? (The music stand and piano area always are, but the rest of the room is often over-looked) Are they sitting too close, so that fortissimo passages make their fillings fall out?

Does the seat end up damp and sweaty from whoever was sitting in it in the lesson before (and the lesson before that, and the lesson before that...)? Leading neatly to...

...does the space itself *smell?* (Anyone who has taught teenage boys who come straight from school—or worse yet, *sports practice*—will know exactly what I mean)

All small details. But they don't feel small when you're a captive audience for 30 minutes—any one of these can make the difference between parents reluctantly dragging themselves out of the chair when the lesson ends, or cutting and running as soon as it's not impolite to do so.

A good test? If the parent is falling asleep during the lesson, it's not a sign that you're dull. It's a sign you've done a great job in making their little space homely.

(At least, that's what I tell myself).

 The **Static Studio** has *somewhere for parents to wait* while the lesson happens. The **Dynamic Studio** creates a *sanctuary for parents to escape* their crazy week for a while

---

What's next:

The scheduling techniques in this chapter are driven by a core Dynamic Studio value: that even the most seemingly unyielding of traditional studio structures can be *pliable*, and re-engineered *in consultation* with students and families.

The next chapter extrapolates this idea of pliability and consultation to another level entirely, and looks at what's possible once students are not just granted consultation or veto rights in lessons, but are actually given *control.*

Dynamic Autonomy

Giving students the illusion of control

Dynamic Autonomy

As ANY EXPERT IN HR WILL tell you, employees who feel as though they have no control over their day-to-day jobs become *unhappy* employees, and unhappy employees *leave*.

It might seem like a strange way to think about your students, but there is an extent to which the power relationship between teacher and student is analogous to that of employer and employee. In the studio, you're the boss: you determine *what* needs to be done, the *urgency* with which those tasks need to be undertaken, the *rewards* for completion, or *penalties* for non-delivery, the *resources* allocated, the *priorities* when those resources are scarce and have (in most studios) *power of veto* over content that represents your business, together with the right to *dismiss*.

Students are therefore very much subject to the calls you make. Of course as a benevolent dictator, you're careful to ensure that your decisions are taken with not only the best interests, but the feelings of your underlings in mind...

...but there are very few managers on the planet who wouldn't say that of themselves. The issue here for the Dynamic Studio is not the *quality* of your decisions, nor the *empathy* with which those determinations are made; it's the crippling *limitations on autonomy* the top-down system imposes on the students themselves.

In short, if you're making all the calls, then students only have one person to blame if they don't like what happens in their lessons. Unhappiness with any element of their lessons inevitably—and logically—manifests as unhappiness with *you*. And like many unhappy employees, they won't necessarily air their concerns; the first warning sign you sometimes get is the fact that they're now an ex-student.

There will be a lot of teachers who disagree with the content of this chapter, but even if the very idea of giving students greater freedom of choice fills you with horror, it's worth at least asking yourself this question as a thought experiment:

What in your studio, *could* you give students control over? How much more invested in their progress, and the studio itself, might they be if they had more input?

> "...if you're making all the calls, then students only have one person to blame if they don't like what happens in their lessons."

Or—more accurately—if they *felt* they had more input. As we'll see, you won't actually be surrendering control. Like so much else about student retention, this is about perceptions; reality doesn't necessarily (and often shouldn't) come along for the ride.

The steering wheel on train tracks

Underpinning this whole idea of empowering students is to ensure that they're selecting from a pre-approved set of options. That way, they get to feel that they're in control of their destiny, while you are still able to carefully manage the way in which their progress unfolds.

This means that nothing in this chapter is suggesting a "so... what do you want to learn today" free-for-all. The lessons would be unmanageable, directionless; most parents would be horrified. Selection from a preset menu gives students the autonomy they seek, while providing a structure that not only avoids anarchy, but ultimately allows you to retain control anyway.

Given that framework, what sorts of decisions could the students be in charge of? What in your studio lends itself to *creating menus* rather than *making announcements?* There are plenty of everyday teaching decisions where this technique could be in play—this chapter looks at some that can make the biggest difference.

Control over the *agenda*

In traditional teaching studios, the teacher is very firmly in charge of *what* the student will be working on, and *when*. They set the pieces, they decide which technical elements will be targeted, and in which order, they decide which themes and concepts to push hard, which to mention in passing, and which to omit entirely.

> "They'll have the satisfaction of knowing that the work they're doing each week is exactly what they asked for."

Obviously the *content* of such decisions is not going to be arbitrary, but the *order* in which they unfold often can be. For example, we might be pushing hard for extending the student's theory development *now*, but honestly, we could equally have deferred it until *later in the year,* or have covered it *last year.* Or we might be working on a technically demanding etude *now*, with a view to balancing it with an adagio movement *once they've finished that.* However, it easily could have been the other way around; the student's development would not have been noticeably accelerated or hindered either way.

Given that, the question of *when* elements are tackled is one that you can often safely throw to your students.

Preparing the agenda (or really, stocking the buffet)

The idea is to list the half-dozen issues/pieces/technical elements/ concepts that you want to cover in the next 12-18 months with the student. You get to decide *what's* on that list, but your student gets to choose the *order* in which you tackle the list items.

The key here is ensuring these options are not dependent on each other in any way. Because you are surrendering control over the order of proceedings, if you have choices on your list which are *prerequisites* for other elements on that same list, then students can end up with problems with horses and carts. So, for example, if a piece on your list requires a student to be comfortable with reading heavily syncopated rhythms, then any drills designed to *prepare* the student to be able to read such rhythms shouldn't be selectable as a separate element. To choose the *piece* is also to choose any *preparation* that might be required—which in this case would be a hefty dose of rhythm reading drills. Common sense, but easily enough overlooked in the enthusiasm of lets-choose-your-own-adventure.

It's also important that you take the time to walk students through exactly what each option would involve, so their decision is informed by the reality of what committing to it would mean. What *new skills* will they be developing from each option? How relatively intense will the between-lesson *preparation* for each will be? How *long* will each option take? Or are some of them an *until-it's-done* kind of module? What does "done" look like? What will their practice look like? Given the student's strengths and weaknesses, how *challenging* are they likely to find each option?

Those cautions aside—and despite the fact that unknown to them, you have long ago vetoed-by-omission much that they otherwise might have requested—most students will relish being asked to choose. They'll be able to defer—or not, as they wish—

the options they're not looking forward to so much, and have the satisfaction of knowing that the work they're doing each week is exactly what they asked for.

And all the while, *you're getting insights into what sorts of lessons they enjoy most.* For any teacher interested in student retention, that's exactly as useful to know as it sounds.

 The **Static Studio** dictates exactly *what* will happen, and *when* it will happen. The **Dynamic Studio** sets out *options*, and lets students *select* from them.

Control of repertoire

Repertoire selection has an enormous bearing on just about every aspect of a student's lessons: the *difficulty* of the piece determines how challenging preparation sessions at home will feel; the *raw appeal* of the piece determines how prepared the student is to want to work on it in the first place, the *extent to which it differs* from repertoire they've already done determines how much groundwork you'll need to lay in lessons, the risk of tedium if the similarities with previous pieces are too great, and the range of new breakthroughs and Achievements they can expect to experience on the journey; the *shape of the learning curve* determines whether this campaign will be easier at the start, and then become steadily more challenging as the piece matures, or some degree of vice-versa; the *frequency* with which this piece has already been represented at studio recitals can determine how enthusiastic students are about joining the ranks of those who've played it (will they *resist* because they pride themselves on being special? Or are they *excited* by the idea of joining the ranks of students who were considered Good Enough To Play This Piece?)

With so much depending on getting repertoire selection right, it might seem foolhardy to place the choice in the hands of someone as inexperienced as a student...but remember, they're selecting from a preapproved list. There's nothing on there that you'd have a problem with them doing; it's similar to the way schools allow students to select subjects—if they don't want students majoring in Brew Your Own Beer 101, then the institution simply wouldn't list it as an option in the first place.

Preparing a portfolio of temptations

Your job here is not just to prepare a mere menu for your students to select from, but a *portfolio of temptations* that will make choosing actively difficult. Your students should feel like they're in one of those rare restaurants where everything on the menu is worth ordering, the choice wracked with the agony of opportunity cost.

This means presenting each work in its best possible light: instead of just titles, students should be able to hear **recordings** of everything on offer, together with some way to **preview** the score (this can be as simple as giving them a CD and a scrapbook of score photocopies, or automated and online, such as the piano repertoire preview section at www.insidemusicteaching.com).

To get them intrigued enough to want to listen to each recording in the first place, it helps to have just a few lines describing each option. But the key here is not to write it as though you're a stuffy musicology lecturer, but as though you are trying to *sell* the idea to your student. (you *are* trying to sell the idea!)

So instead of:

> **Etude in C.** Moderate to Advanced. Harmonically ambiguous, with the driving rhythms that are characteristic of Dortmuller's early works...

I fell asleep while I was *writing* that; no student is going to read it. Try this instead:

> **Insanely fast showstopper!** This Etude in C amazes audiences whenever they hear it—there's *so* much packed into just 50 seconds. For brave students only.

Similarly, instead of:

> **Reverie:** Flowing contrapuntal Lydian mode melodies, with quotations from popular songs of the 1890s.

Well, that's really going to fire up your students...popular songs from the *1890s*, holy heck...ok, so after a makeover:

> **Create a dreamscape:** You'll need control and imagination to bring this Reverie to life. One of the most beautiful pieces on any list this year.

The students just need to be curious enough to want to hear the recordings—from there the pieces can speak for themselves, but the student's thinking will have been shaped in advance by your carefully worded copy. They'll be picturing the Etude in terms of being a *showstopper*, they'll be looking for the Reverie to be *unusually beautiful*...the positive first impressions have already been established, and the student is yet to hear a single note.

Remember, your job is not to describe the pieces comprehensively, or with New Grove accuracy. You're just trying to get students curious enough to actually listen to the work. If it really is important for them to understand that those 1890s flowing melodies are rooted in Lydian mode, then that's a point you can make when teaching the piece is well underway; make that fact a highlight up front, and they might not care enough to choose the piece in the first place.

It's *their* piece

Having been *assigned* a piece is very different—and much less motivating—than having *chosen* one. This is then not a piece that they're dutifully doing because they were informed it's What's Next. This is a piece they're working on because they effectively window-shopped for it. Nobody should be surprised if the practice that follows is a lot more plentiful and engaged than would have been otherwise.

The **Static Studio** *assigns pieces* like a doctor prescribes medication. The **Dynamic Studio** *showcases repertoire options* like a five-star restaurant menu lists dishes.

Control over workload intensity

As a blood-pressure monitor attached to any music teacher or student would confirm, the demands of music lessons are not constant. Some weeks we send students home staggering under the weight of a teetering intray, other weeks can feel more like a holding pattern of light maintenance-only practice.

There's nothing wrong with this sort of variability—one idea in Chapter 2 (➡34‑36) even went so far as to *recommend* that the studio workload not be allowed to settle into anything too predictable—but problems can quickly arise if the peaks and troughs of your requirements align badly with those imposed elsewhere in the student's life. Coincide your heaviest demands too often with similarly tough workloads in other areas of your students life—whether by accident or design—and you're well on the way to losing that student. This has never been more true than with today's students, who are often overcommitted even before their very first lesson.

One way to ensure better studio-student workload alignment is to start a regular conversation about it by creating a *scale* of Workload Intensity. The idea is that any week that is rated as a "1" is very light, while a "10" is all stops out, cancel everything, no-time-for-meals-or-sleep, this week is *all* about music. The existence of the scale doesn't change reality at all, it just gives teacher and student a common language to start accommodating it with.

You can then, for example, warn your students that because you want to spend some time soon looking at techniques for getting pieces ready despite impossibly tight deadlines (a skill *every* musician needs), two of the weeks in this Semester need to be a 9...but your students are allowed to nominate in advance *which* two weeks. This means they can scan their calendar for testing weeks at school, or play rehearsals—weeks that are already an 8 or a 9 in their own right—and then schedule your requested 9s *around* those.

To offset this, you might also have a couple of weeks which will be very light—say a 2 or a 3, with next to no practice expected—again the student would be allowed to look at the rest of their commitments and work out when those weeks most usefully (and safely) could be.

This, of course, is mutually exclusive of that idea outlined in Chapter 2, where the whole point was to occasionally *surprise* your student with unexpectedly heavy or light weeks. (A lot of the ideas outlined in this book are mutually exclusive...God forbid than any teacher should try to implement *all* of them) But if the timing of the week that demands a 9 is not to be *sprung* on a student as a challenge, but *predetermined*, then it might as well be predetermined by the student.

> The **Static Studio** pushes the student's accelerator and brake for them.
> The **Dynamic Studio** allows the student to drive to the conditions.

Control over closure

Because pieces can always be improved, it can be maddeningly difficult to know when it's time to move on to what's next. Most works are subject to the same laws of diminishing returns that any expertise development is; normally what happens is that the teacher will make the call as to when it's Enough Already.

We don't always get this right. Often we'll keep pieces past their best-before date because we can still find improvements that could be made. But what we often miss in the process is that the student has long since tired of the work, and that each incremental refinement now is coming at the cost of falling enthusiasm levels.

It's rare that we're obtuse enough to get this wrong for months on end. But it's not unusual at all to keep pieces on life-support a fortnight or two longer than they should have been. That's a handful of lessons that were draining the student of positive thoughts about music lessons, and that easily could have been used for something else...if only we'd known.

So ask. Just as it's useful to have an 1-10 index of Workload Intensity, it's also useful to have a similar scale for How Fired Up Are You Still About This Piece. When that score hits 2 or 3, you *have* to know, and you might not if you don't actively fish for it.

Don't misunderstand me here. I'm not proposing that students be allowed to abandon pieces at the first sign of resistance; all too often that can be the first time that they are having *genuine problems* with the piece. But if the weariness is caused instead by the fact that *the well seems to be running dry*—that the student simply cannot see how the incrementally small improvements left are worth the enormous investment of time required to realise them, then you need to know.

At that point, you've got two options. You either have to sell the importance of the remaining changes—not merely mandate those changes, but convince the student that they're worth making—or you have to give the student permission to move on.

If you're not confident of the former, then you need to move quickly to the latter; the most effective way to do that is to make it the student's call:

> Listen, you've done some great work on this Sonata over the past few months—there are still some minor improvements that I think would help it, but I'm concerned that the amount of practice required might cut badly into other things we could be working on. I'll take you through what I see those improvements as being, but it's then up to you as to whether we push through a little more, or call time on this right now.

Over to them.

Do students sometimes leave because they're forced to work on pieces long after those pieces start to smell bad? Yes. Many, many times. It's not going to happen in *your* studio though.

The **Static Studio** knows when it's time to stop a piece. The **Dynamic Studio** knows that they often *don't* know.

Creative control

This can be a tough issue for music teachers to concede, but students having autonomy over how they play is ultimately what we're preparing them for in any case. The question here is not one of whether such control should be ceded, but how much, and how early.

For student retention purposes, and for today's students in particular, the answer needs to be "more than you'd like" and "sooner than feels comfortable".

The reason is that while the tension between *sensitivity to the dictates of the score* and *freedom to create your own performance* is a fundamental struggle for any musician, highly creative students in particular can feel smothered by any hint of here's-the-one-true-way-to-play-this.

This wouldn't be so concerning, except for the fact that much of traditional teaching is necessarily based on reining students in; on issuing corrections that reflect where and how the student has diverged from score-informed orthodoxy: why are you *getting louder* here when there is *no crescendo marked?* Where are the *staccatos* in your phrasing that are *clearly marked* in measures 24-38?

But for some students, being free to not only liberally interpret, but sometimes *actively override* score markings is a big part of what drives their enjoyment of playing in the first place; such students prefer to regard score markings as recommendations rather than gospel, and like Baz Luhrmann directing Shakespeare, can produce interpretations that are classically unthinkable, but oddly compelling nonetheless.

> "...autonomy over how they play is ultimately what we're preparing them for in any case."

When confronted with such students, you can either force compliance, or accommodate and then bring out the best that lies within the unorthodoxy. The former will help your studio achieve a certain consistency whenever your students perform in competitions, but will also—and you are kidding yourself if you think otherwise—cost you students along the way.

You may well decide that this price is worth the consistency and orthodoxy that would result. That's fine. This book is, after all, a compendium of possibilities; you'd end up with a very strange studio indeed if you were to adopt all of them simultaneously, and without question.

The **Static Studio** is a *curator*; their prime responsibility is to the correct performance of each piece. The **Dynamic Studio** is a *director* whose prime responsibility is to get the most out of each actor.

Control over the extent of participation

Most studios host flagship events that come with—let me just read here what this standard studio policy has to say on the matter—*non-negotiable universal participation requirements*. Translated into parent-speak: every student plays in every studio recital, every time, no exceptions.

Now there's no doubting the benefit policies like this can bring to a studio. Mandatory performances are how teachers ensure that studio events feel suitably large-scale; all students present, cheering and waving the studio flag, our version of a May Day Parade.

As a studio retention tactic though, it's a one-size-fits-all disaster: forcing a genuinely performance-phobic student to prepare for a Big Studio Recital because "everyone has to" ranks right up there with asking an arachnophobic student to sit still while you tip a bucket of spiders on their head. It's a silly, entirely preventable reason to have a student dreading their lessons.

Now before I start getting complaints about resultant half-empty studio recitals, we're not talking here about accommodating those students whose problem is *inertia*, or mere *reluctance*—nudging students like that onstage can be transformative for them, and produce some of your proudest teaching moments. Instead we're limiting—but also insisting on—exceptions for those whose thoughts turn to grave-diggers and Room 101 when they even *think* about performing in public: the fact that the performance might have been *good for them*, or *character building*, or *helping their confidence* is a moot point if they quit lessons entirely just to avoid the trauma.

Opening up exceptions like this though leaves many music teachers with an existential problem: if the student doesn't perform, then what are lessons *for?*

We'll count the ways in a moment, but while there are a lot of music teachers who reject the idea, learning to *play* an instrument does *not* necessarily require learning how to *perform*. There's no rule that says you're not progressing unless you're prepared to do the musical equivalent of public speaking.

In the meantime, compulsory participation not only gives performance-phobic students *a reason to quit*, it also gives them a *deadline*. When was that Huge Concert In Front Of The Whole Studio again? December 3? Noted. Gives me four months to get out of here...

It probably wouldn't sell many copies, but if I were writing a book on how to *lose* students, I'd recommend the following Static Studio solution: find your most insecure, fearful, uncomfortable-in-front-of-crowds students, and then subject them to *exactly the same* performance demands that are designed to bring out the best in your most confident, capable and eager students. You'll have extra spare time in no time.

If not performing, then...what?

Excusing a student from a performance requirement doesn't mean removing all expectations and goals—there are endless alternatives: performance phobic students can, for example, still make *recordings*, or work towards a whole string of *lesson based achievements,* or become the student in your studio who *knows more about theory than anyone else*, or who can *play anything by ear,* or who is *first to master all their scales*, or who *engineers dynamics and rubato solutions* for students who are playing in the recital, or any number of other alternative goals that would give them an opportunity to *shine*, rather than merely *survive*.

In that mix, there's nothing stopping you from a little managed exposure therapy to address the performance phobia too. Maybe they have to play their piece in front of their parents to earn 5 points, a friend to earn 10, a random student from the studio and both his or her parents for 20 points. All orders of magnitude below a full blown studio recital, while keeping alive the possibility that one day their name might feature in the program too.

The dynamic studio principle at play here is not which alternative to choose, it's that an alternative—in fact, many alternatives—are available. The first step to this sort of differentiation is to give students the power of veto over recital participation; not to be exercised lightly, or without discussion, but always heeded—and then taken as an invitation to find substitute goals and Achievements.

The **Static Studio** has flagship events that are the focal point for the *entire studio*
The **Dynamic Studio** has additional and alternative focal points, differentiated for *individual students.*

Control over the feedback process

Music teaching by its very nature is about troubleshooting. There are tempos to correct, wrong notes to be tidied up, intonation to improve, rhythms to tighten; where a disparity exists between the student's current performance and what the score asks for, conscientious teachers will work tirelessly to narrow the gap.

This model becomes a problem once we cross a fine line, and are not working with the *student*, but instead *the performance itself*—as if it were an entity that existed independently of the person playing it.

A good illustration of this principle at work—of how it's entirely possible to give excellent feedback without needing to refer to the student at all—is the inner critic that inevitably emerges when you hear a work for your instrument on the radio. You won't necessarily know who is playing, and therefore

> "Slogging through a perpetually regenerating todo list that someone else is creating is a horribly demotivating way to work"

anything at all about the performer, but that's not a prerequisite to forming your own judgements about the performance itself: you'll be perfectly able to observe that the *cadenza* has been taken way too fast, or that *this melodic line* gets lost, or that the *fugue subject entries* are being brought out like they've been hit by nailguns.

Despite the fact that the performer was effectively behind a curtain—nameless, faceless, generic—the transcript of the comments you were able to give would have been eerily reminiscent of transcripts of feedback we give actual, live, human students during lessons.

...your cadenza is too fast. The melodic line is getting lost. The fugue subject entries are being overplayed.

Of course, all these things have to be said. We can't have the student taking the cadenza at breakneck speed, or burying the melodic line, or belting every fugue subject entry. But the focus of all that feedback is on the *piece*, not the *student*.

In a profession based upon relationships, this manner of relating—not of teacher-to-student, but teacher-to-*piece*—is toxic, particularly if it becomes the default.

Now before you dismiss this as something that only happens to other (obviously more unfeeling and clueless) teachers, consider how often your feedback sounds like this:

{

The **pianissimo section** needs to project more.

Those **eighth notes** are not even.

That **crescendo** needs to be more dramatic.

That **fingering** is not going to work.

The **trill** needs to be longer.

There needs to be a **breath between these phrases.**

The elements targeted in such criticisms will vary, but we've *all* given instructions that at least *rhyme* with these. It's how we get (in this instance) projecting pianissimos, even eighth notes, dramatic crescendos, correct fingering, phrasing that breathes; it's the very stuff of teaching, and we've got hundreds of excellent studio recital performances to prove: *it works*.

Conspicuously absent though in such laundry lists of corrections is the *student*: from the transcript alone of requested corrections, it's not possible to discern their gender, or age, or interests, or learning preferences, or what makes them laugh, or whether perhaps their parent was in the room. The student is an agent invisible, responsible for rendering the requested corrections, but in this instance otherwise not really necessary; the train driver in a conversation that is entirely about the train.

Put like that, the whole process doesn't sound like much fun for the student.

It's not. Slogging through a perpetually regenerating todo list that someone else is creating is a horribly demotivating way to work, specially if you're someone who needs *creative input*, or *options*, or the *feeling of being in control*, all traits of some of the most exciting, rewarding students in any studio, but also of students who are most likely to be miserable when their scope for input feels at all like paint-by-number.

An impasse then. To do our job, there are inevitably lists of changes that we need to work through, but the very act of methodically working through them can hit our ability to retain some of our best and brightest.

The solution becomes clear when you consider this: *you're not the only person in the room who is able to spot problems and recommend solutions.* It turns out that even giving feedback—the most fundamental of teaching tasks—can usefully be ceded to the people we teach.

Let's take a look at the different degrees to which this is possible:

Lvl 1: Student to choose between *prelisted agenda items*

This is the most basic of the put-the-student-in-charge-of-corrections techniques, and again, the control is an illusion.

The idea is that you present the student with your list of what needs fixing—the student gets no say over what's on that list, but they do get to choose the *order* in which those issues are tackled. So there might be one that's related to *fingering*, another to *choice of tempo* for the coda, another to their *legato playing* and one more to a *reading error*...sorry, what did you ask for? Reading error first? Sure, let's take a look...

From there, it's still your change that will be implemented, but the student got to choose which door to look behind. It's a simple change to make, but already is helping stop the feedback-based lesson from feeling like one-way traffic; they're more likely to feel that this was not just *your* corrections, but *theirs too*.

Lvl 2: Student chooses between *prelisted solutions*

A variation on this is to dictate the problem that is to be solved, but cede control over which solution to use. So for example you might tell the student that the *tempo* in the development section needs to be *better controlled*, but then give them

> "In a profession based upon relationships, this manner of relating—not of teacher-to-student, but teacher-to-*piece*—is toxic"

several different ways of dealing with the problem. They can try any, some, or all of whatever is on your list...as long as the outcome of the controlled tempo is met, you don't mind how they got there.

Not only does this start to give the student some genuine autonomy over the feeding and watering of their piece, but it also gives them experience in working with multiple solutions to a single problem...all of which is excellent preparation for the next stage of student autonomy...

Lvl 3: Student to *recommend solutions*

Extended the previous techniques further is to propose no solutions at all, but to simply *state* the problem:

the opening lacks impact

and then have the student hypothesizing and then testing

their own solutions. So with this particular stated issue, they might come back to you with suggestions that they try a version of the opening that is *20 bpm faster*; they might look at *more biting staccatos*; they might consider *greater dynamic range*; they might try *abandoning dynamic range entirely* and generating tension by keeping things very, very quiet; they might run the passage with *more vibrato*, or *less*; they might abandon taking the usual settling time before they begin the performance, and simply *launch* into the piece, hoping to catch the audience off-balance; they might choose to *exaggerate the space between the phrases*, creating more of a sense of mystery, or they might have the whole thing *sitting breathlessly on the front edge of the beat...* all worth trying, all focused on the problem you stated, and most importantly, all suggested by the student. Test drive the options, lock in what works best. This isn't then just an opening with more impact: it's a problem they've solved themselves.

The whole process is similar to the way in which parents help learner drivers: the parent is right there, but their teenager is steering; guided autonomy, if you will.

Lvl 4: Student to come up with their own issues and solutions

This is the ultimate in granting students control, although even here, that control can be somewhat more of an illusion than the student suspects, depending on how much stock you place in your ability to subliminally or otherwise influence your student's thinking.

The technique works best if you've got some way of recording the student, and then are able to play it back right there in the lesson (➡ 261)—that way, they can *hear* exactly what they just played, and can *generate their own list* of what needs fixing, together with their *own solutions* to those problems.

The key to retaining some control here is that the list of what needs fixing is not going to be arrived at in a vacuum—it will come after a discussion, and you can definitely lead this witness. So if you're hoping that *tempo control* is prominent on their list, then you can seed that by asking a question in the discussion phase:

"I just want to check something—can I get you use the metronome to figure out how fast the opening is going"

Of course, you've got no interest here in how fast the opening is. What you are interested in is the fact that the variable tempo is going to make finding a tempo to lock the metronome to impossible—shortly after their metronome tempo-check starts, the student should find themselves blaming the "crazy speed changes" they can hear in the recording...

...from there, they can make their own conclusions.

Notice, yet again: they're still ending up where you were hoping they'd go, it's just that they'll feel like they discovered it for themselves.

(Mwuhahaha...there is *no escaping* your will...even when they think they're free to apply theirs...*cue thunderclap and organ music*)

The **Static Studio** *points out* all the problems, and then *comes up with* all the solutions.
The **Dynamic Studio** helps student *scout* for problems, and then *experiment* to discover their own solutions.

Control over their practice week

I've covered this issue in much more depth in my other books, but there are few issues in music lessons that cause such grief—and such compelling reasons to abandon lessons—as problems with practicing.

The good news is that if practice is what's making students miserable, there is plenty of scope for improvement. There are many, many alternatives to how your students currently work (*Practiceopedia* details over 350 pages of options), but for student retention purposes *how* they work is not nearly as important as ensuring that student feels like they have *ownership* over that work.

For this reason, the prescriptive practice instructions that so often appear at the end of lessons are not nearly as helpful as they might first seem. Take the following well-meaning example:

> **This week:** Twenty minutes of scales every day, followed by ten minutes of work on your Sonatina. Use the rest of the time to get Elephant Blues up to speed.

For reasons that the *Practice Revolution* goes into in much more depth, these are terrible practice instructions, but for student retention purposes the relevant problem here is that the instructions mandate *how much time* the student needs to spend on *what*. This will leave some students feeling like a worker on an assembly line—do *this* for *this* long, then *that*, then *this*, don't *argue*—there's no ownership over the final product, no capacity for them to determine how best to get the job done, no variety, no respite. No point. Practice is a predetermined, automated, eyes-glaze-over soulless snow-covered path to be shovelled.

Much better is to forget about dictating *how much* and *what*, and simply to give students a desired *outcome*:

Your goal: to be able to start next lesson by playing F major scale three times in a row, clean, correct fingering, eighth notes at 100 bpm.

And if you want **Student Of The Week points?** 5 times in a row, at *120* bpm. 1 bonus point for every 5 bpm over that!

This small change in what's asked for sets things up for a completely different experience at home. You've said nothing about *how much* practice they have to do each day, *how* to get the job done, or *which order* to work on things. You've just defined what success looks like, together with some dangled incentives to extend themselves even further.

Some students are entirely happy to take everything from there, in which case the best way to help them is to get out of their way. Others will drown in the absence of further directions, and will need help with how to get the job done; again though, you don't have to cage even those students with prescriptive instructions. To give them help *and* ownership over the week ahead, even your guidance can be in the form of *options* to choose between:

Suggested practice techniques: *Chaining*, *Metronome Method*, *Bugspotting*, *Cementing* and a *Stripped Score* to make sure you're clear on the fingering. Consider also setting up a *Pressure Test* and *Lesson Preflight Check* to ensure you're as ready as you think you are.

These are all techniques that are detailed in *Practiceopedia*, but you can substitute with whatever you happen to use in your own studio. Note the use of the word "suggested" though: the point is that none of your listed techniques would be compulsory for the student; they're options for the student to consider.

The message? *This is your campaign. You're in charge of the strategy. I trust you.*

To ensure the student doesn't just drift though, the message also contains: *Next lesson starts with a test that you need to be ready for.*

And so, as for so many of the other techniques in this chapter, the freedom and control you're giving is largely illusory. In this case, the student didn't get to choose *what* their job is—next lesson will be starting with that scales test, come what may, and they have to suit up for it. But they do get to choose *when* to practice, *how much*, and *what form* that practice takes, whether their campaign should be based around a *single practice technique drilled hard*, or whether to use *several*.

They can also tailor their work at home to meet the demands of the rest of their week, the time they have available for particular practice sessions, their energy levels, and their preferred methods for getting the job done. In our list above, Metronome Method is a very different technique for speeding things up than Chaining: students who need *a taste of success with the final tempo now* almost always prefer the latter, those who prefer *measurable evidence of steady progress* are happier with the former. The point is not that one is better than the other; the point is that they were able to choose their favourite, which in turn makes they're practice more enjoyable and productive.

Set against this is that they know they're accountable for reaching the goal you set. There are consequences for not being ready; scaling rewards if you meet, and then exceed expectations.

So...all students should have options like this?

This far into the book, it should be clear that the answer is no: *the big enemy of student retention is universal solutions forced onto a studio of individual needs.* Some students will respond best if they have a run sheet for every practice session mapped out in advance: so be it. Others won't even need a list of options to choose between—all they need to hear is the goal for the week, and they can take it from there. If you're interested in keeping both types of students, then you need to allow for both types of practice structures.

In short, if anyone were to ask you "what expectations do you have of how students should practice", and you answer with anything other than "it depends; which student did you have in mind?", then somewhere, every day, and probably right now, what's happening in the practice room is probably costing you students.

The **Static Studio** expects students to do a *set amount of practice* every day.
The **Dynamic Studio** expects students to complete *set challenges* each week.

What's next:

This chapter has been about giving students a sense of *control* over their journey through your studio; the next is about ensuring they have a clear and constantly updating sense of *progress* along the way.

It's about making the shift from a studio that *gives positive reinforcement* (Well done! What a clever student! What a pretty hat!) to one that *highlights achievements*. (Here's what you can do today that you couldn't do yesterday.), so that all those accolades actually *mean* something...

...and so they can tell their lessons are *working*.

Dynamic Scoreboards
Relentless, engaging evidence of *progress*

Dynamic Scoreboards

MUSIC TEACHERS HAVE KNOWN FOR A long time that students who *aren't progressing* are students in *danger of leaving*. The Static Studio response to this is to work harder to make sure students continue to improve.

Unfortunately *making sure students continue to improve* is missing the point entirely. It's not students who are stalled we need to worry about, it's students who *think* they're stalled. The actual rate of progress is irrelevant; it's the perception that is key.

The failure here is one of communication, as the teacher and student look at exactly the same lessons through entirely different lenses. There are two reasons in particular that the teacher's perspective is not likely to align with that of their students:

First of all, when teachers are looking for forward movement, the focus tends to be on *developmental* progress—breakthroughs that can unlock the big What's Next as we teach. This would be fine, except that such breakthroughs are *pedagogical* milestones, often too abstract, sophisticated and subtle for the student to even be aware of, much less excited by. In other words, they're our breakthroughs, not theirs.

The second is that as adults with years of musical training, we usually have a very different perspective over what constitutes "stalled" as opposed to what is merely "acceptably steady development". To today's students, who are so used to things happening *fast*, the latter looks exactly like the former.

So instead of asking "Is Julia progressing?" and then congratulating yourself as you think about just how far she's come since those early lessons, you should be asking a very different question:

How can Julia *tell* she's progressing?

What *evidence* is there available to her? How *clearly and engagingly* is that evidence presented? How *long has it been* since she would have last seen such evidence?

This chapter is all about making sure you—and your students—have got answers to those questions.

Making progress visible

Thanks to a trip I once endured through a tropical storm in a Fokker—during which even the cabin crew were strapped down and kissing photos of their families—I now hate flying with a passion, and will continue to avoid it wherever possible until Boeing makes a QE2 sized plane that is turbulence-proof, can get me from Sydney to London in 25 minutes, and flies six feet off the ground the whole way. (I keep checking the Boeing website. They don't seem to have this one in production yet.) However, on those rare occasions where flying is unavoidable, one of the things that helps keep me sane is the map that comes up with GPS updates of our location; it means that every half hour or so, I can look up and see that we're actually progressing—the little plane seemed to be *south* of Fiji last time I checked, and now it seems *level*. That's *good*, we're *getting there*.

Of course, at an abstract level, I know there's constant progress—we're hurtling forwards in this vacuum-sealed death tube at almost 1,000 km/h—but there's something about the chart-like visual that gives a greater sense of actually getting somewhere.

The point here is that creating the *perception* of progress is an entirely different task from creating the *progress itself*; it's as different as the *chart* of the plane is from the *actual* plane.

Where can your students look to see evidence of their own progress? Is there a chart of some sort that gets added to? A book? Badges? Stickers? A webpage? Cards they get to collect? A change to what they can wear to lessons? An honour board their name gets added to? A growing timeline with marked highlights? A new class they qualify for? A video-highlights reel? A checklist with Achievements to tick off? An *app* with a checklist with Achievements to tick off? A set of miniature trophies to collect? An entry in the Big Studio Book Of Heroes? A summary in a report? A public chronicle of their achievements before their performance at the end-of-year recital?

> "Instead of asking "*is* Julie progressing", you should be asking "how can Julie *tell* she's progressing?""

Remember, I'm not talking about the reflex and ephemeral "well done!" kind of feedback here. I'm talking about something more permanent: a genuine and growing compendium of the their Achievements, their Breakthroughs, their Milestones. Somewhere, for example, that records the date they *first played this piece from memory.* Or that they *moved on from Book 2 to Book 3.* Or that they *performed in their first recital.* Or that they've just performed in their *10th.*

Something that shows them that this plane is moving forward, past interesting and noteworthy landmarks, and moving forward *fast.*

The **Static Studio** teaches from *semester* to *semester*, and makes sure students know the start and end dates. The **Dynamic Studio** teaches from *breakthrough* to *breakthrough*, and makes sure students can name exactly what these breakthroughs were.

The bluewater problem

There is one drawback with the map-based progress chart on the plane. Because I'm generally flying to or from Australia, a lot of the journey is over the ocean, and landmarks like *Fiji* or *Hawaii* or *Guam* are few and far between. If the map is zoomed in at all, often all I can see is a plane on a featureless expanse of blue—which is exactly all I can see when I look out the window...and exactly what I saw an hour ago as well—and now my updates all look alike.

With no point of reference, not only do these updates fail to give evidence of progress, they can actually give the unsettling sensation that there *is* no progress.

The nature of music lessons is largely for gradual improvement, punctuated by occasional dramatic breakthroughs. This means that whatever evidence-of-progress medium you choose to use to record all these high points, the problem you can quickly run into is a lack of material. There just aren't many islands, and there's a lot of water.

The important principle here for the Dynamic Studio is to be prepared to think more laterally—and liberally— about what should constitute a landmark in the first place. If all you do is mark Capital-A Achievements such as *graduating from Book 1 to Book 2*, or *winning a competition*, then evidence of progress can be months apart. That's *not* going to cut it for students used to moving at the speed of optic fibre.

But if you're prepared to *subdivide* these Capital-A Achievements—and then possibly even subdivide those subdivisions—then suddenly you're in complete control over *how many* achievements there are, and *how widely* they're spaced—which means you can match the frequency with which evidence of progress is given to the needs of the student.

So, for the student working their way through Book 1, rather than waiting the eight months for the Book 2 graduation moment, you could zoom in, and list each of the *sections* of the book as a series of landmarks in their own right. These landmarks might be spaced a few months apart; now the student has three progress milestones instead of just one.

For a different student who needs more frequent reassurance, zoom in further still, and you could be heralding the completion of individual pieces, and now landmarks are separated by just weeks. Zoom further still for a different (probably very young) student, and you're marking several weekly milestones *within* each piece: the occasion that the student could *first play through Page 1 of The Lost Cow at tempo*, or when they *first listened to the recording*, or when they tracked down and *watched 10 different performances of the piece on YouTube*, or when they could *first tap the rhythm of the melody* in its entirety.

Now instead of the journey through Book 1 being marked by a single entry in their Book of Achievements—or their Webpage of Highlights, or StickerSheet of Awesomeness, or however it is that you choose to record the breakthroughs—you've been able to give the student a *steady drip* of progress confirmation. For a student like this, it should be rare that they get through a lesson without you recording something.

What if the lesson genuinely was an Achievement-free zone?

It doesn't need to *seem* that way. You have to be careful not to devalue the entire Achievement currency, but it's worth thinking laterally to still ensure *something* genuinely positive gets mentioned.

So, for example, even if their entire lesson consisted of the student messing up the same underpracticed section over and over, it's still possible to make lemonade from these lemons.

They key element in this example—and pretty much the only thing you've got to work with—is "over and over again". So:

April 18: The Iron Will Award.

Hollbeck Etude in F, Page 2—Tricky passage that was particularly tough after being left out of Alex's practice week...but not tough enough to make him surrender: 50 times the passage knocked him down, 50 times he got back up. Awesome.

Questions about the value of playing something incorrectly 50 times in a row notwithstanding, note that we didn't ignore the elephant in the room here: if Alex hadn't practiced the week before, then that needs to be acknowledged. It was. However *lecturing* him about what a mess the piece is is not going to motivating him to work better this week. Making him *proud* of something he did today just might though.

Note also that while the evidence of genuine progress here is thin at best, it's also not an undeserved accolade: this student *did* keep getting back up, despite the passage defeating him 50 times in a row, and that's worth celebrating. Any Dynamic Studio depends on the list of things students are proud of to be growing noticeably and regularly, but also for those students to have genuinely earned whatever positives are chronicled—handling an otherwise bad week in this fashion achieves both.

The **Static Studio** *waits* for breakthroughs that are significant enough to be worth highlighting. The **Dynamic Studio** *reveals* breakthroughs that the student didn't even know were there.

Turning selected breakthroughs into a Studio Highlights Reel

With so many achievements and breakthroughs being recorded in the studio every week, you'll have plenty of milestones to cherry-pick from and then highlight for your whole studio to see.

So while a lot of studios will have a *Student of the Week* type award, a comprehensive record of student achievements will allow you to have *Breakthroughs of the Week* instead:

10 lessons in a row without forgetting any books
Lauren Carter

Scales Challenge: Level 3 complete!
Alberto Duiz; now blitzing his way through Level 4

1st Public Performance
Nagwa Fahim, at her Year 5 recital at school.

Tempo Breakthrough
Sandra Kask: Czerny etude is now at 130 bpm, more than double what she started at.

YouTube Performance
Seo-Ho Jun: Excellent performance of *Jeux d'eau*, recorded and uploaded during Wednesday's lesson.

What's key here is that the *focus is on the achievements themselves*, rather than the names of the students who earned them. The point of this reversal is for the list to serve as inspiration for ways students could be earning achievements of their own, rather than simply being a roll-call of the names of This Week's Superstars; the former is of interest to everyone, the latter only to those receiving the accolade.

For parents, it's also an ongoing catalogue of the difference that music lessons can make, while the very existence of such lists confirms that yours is a busy, achievement-centred studio, where many, many small victories are won every day.

The **Static Studio** acknowledges *names*.
The **Dynamic Studio** celebrates *achievements*.

Advance flagging achievements

While the acknowledgement of a completed achievement is one of the most meaningful encouragements you can give any student, as any computer game developer will tell you, achievements can actually do most of their best work *before* they've been awarded.

We'll be looking in the chapter on Dynamic Rewards (➡ 229) at the value of a structure of *earnable* rewards, where criteria are clearly set in advance, and any student can qualify simply by ticking all the boxes. However *advance flagging* achievements works a little differently, in that it's much more responsive and fluid: rather than predefining an entire set of awards and their associated criteria, an opportunity for a flagged achievement is likely to appear *spontaneously*, in response to something that you've spotted in a lesson, and couldn't have anticipated otherwise.

So, for example, your student might be having difficulty reproducing an unconventional fingering in an extended scales passage. Instead of just urging them onwards by asking them to "try it again" or "please practice it this week", turn it into a challenge, with a clear and measurable picture of what success looks like:

> Ok, here's one we'll post straight to your Achievements Book, once you can do it: Half tempo—*this* passage—three times in a row, with the fingering we've marked. Nail that with no mistakes, and we'll mark it down as a highlight. Do you want to try that today, or do you want to tackle it next lesson instead?

Note the false dilemma at the end. Without actually dictating that the student *must* be able to do this, you've set up this challenge as a focal point, with no frictionless way for the student to avoid it. They do have a choice though: if the student doesn't want to spend time this week practicing it, then they need to be able to get their head together enough to complete the challenge now. Otherwise, they'll need to structure their practice this week partly around suiting up for that challenge next week.

Either way, for them to actually complete this spontaneously germinated challenge *requires a change in how they were approaching a problem*—not any easy thing for any person to do, musician or otherwise. When this ends up being marked in the book as a milestone, you're not just handing out lollies at a birthday party— they've *earned* this, and should remember it well when they look back over their achievements at the end of the year.

 **Static Studio** awards are only *recognised retrospectively*. **Dynamic Studio** awards are *seeded in advance*.

The review of the Year that Was

The focus on recording regular, measurable achievements means that in the course of a 40 week teaching year, students should rack up a sizeable collection of official accomplishments.

It's worth pausing in the final lesson of the year, and doing a roll-call of just what those breakthroughs were—all the more so if the parents can be there too. It might take most of the lesson simply to run through the list, but it's time well spent: you're making very clear just how many different ways the student has moved forwards in the past 12 months.

It's very hard for the student then to hit that extended break with doubts about whether they're actually accomplishing anything in their lessons—the evidence of progress has just been laid bare; every triumph from the Year That Was reprised.

Reinforce this by cherry picking some of those achievements to highlight again as you introduce the student at their recital, or again in a student profile in a studio newsletter, and they'll be positively marinating in evidence that their lessons are *making a difference.*

As soon as a student can honestly say that, the otherwise constant pressure of what-else-could-I-be-doing starts to ease, and you're well on the way to keeping them.

Better still, that impressive list of achievements from *this* year then seeds a question: how many breakthroughs await them *next* year? You're not the only one who'll be wondering, and then itching to find out.

The **Static Studio** wouldn't waste valuable lesson time recapping highlights from *this* year. The **Dynamic Studio** knows that such recaps make it more likely that there will be a *next* year.

Choosing repertoire with milestones in mind

Like almost every other aspect of teaching, an achievement-based feedback system is actually highly dependent on the repertoire that students are assigned.

In the absence of such achievement-based systems, there are normally three considerations that weigh particularly heavily when teachers choose repertoire:

1) The pedagogical value of the content. To what extent does it support my current and future teaching strategies with this student?

2) The student's own preferences. How *excited* will they be about studying this piece?

3) External requirements. Is this piece somehow mandatory, or tick necessary boxes for an upcoming examination or competition?

But if your studio is making a switch to regularly and proactively acknowledging breakthroughs and achievements, then it's worth adding a fourth.

4) How rich is this piece with opportunities to find new Achievements for the student to earn?

To answer this question, you need to look at the piece in an entirely new way:

Does it contain identifiably *new techniques?* Would playing this piece *from memory* be a significant challenge, worthy of an achievement in its own right? Does it contain notes that go *beyond the student's existing range?* Is the tempo demanding enough to open up the possibility of a series of *tempo-based milestones?* Is this piece perhaps in a *key the student has not worked with before?* Is it *longer* than any other piece they've tried so far? Or short enough that you might be able to chase a *learn-it-in-a-week* type of achievement? Is it their very first piece of this *genre*—their first etude, or fugue, or rondo? Does it *divide neatly* into clearly defined and contrasting sections, making it suitable for segment-based Achievements? Are they the *first student in the studio*—ever—to play this piece? Or the *youngest?* Or the first who has been learning *less than a year* to attempt it? How readily might the path to mastering this piece be *segmented* and *signposted?*

> "...you'll be able parse a piece for potential milestones just as quickly and easily as you currently do for technical issues, or key signature changes."

Repertoire looks very different when considered with milestones in mind; after a while you'll be able parse a musical score for potential milestones just as quickly and easily as you currently do for technical issues, or key signature changes.

It's not going to happen, but personally, I'd like to see pieces come with Milestone Potential rating labels, just like electrical appliances come with energy-saver ratings. You won't believe how much easier your job is—and how many more reasons you can create for a student to look forward to their practice—with a 5 star piece.

The **Static Studio** looks for breakthroughs in repertoire students are working on *right now*. The **Dynamic Studio** *vets upcoming repertoire* specifically with breakthroughs in mind.

Keeping a breakthroughs diary

This technique is outlined in detail in a chapter of its own in *Practiceopedia*, but there's no reason that it has to be limited just to practice. The basic idea of the *Practiceopedia* version is that students would keep a practice diary each day, recording not how much practice they did (don't start me on what a soul-destroying, lesson-wrecking, progress-sabotaging focus that is), but what they achieved. Were they able to play this passage *from memory for the very first time?* Or another passage at *75% of the full tempo?* Or did they finally *work out a fingering* for that tricky section on page 4?

> **"...in short, what could they do *today* that they couldn't do *yesterday?*"**

In short, what could they do today that they couldn't do yesterday?

It's a powerful technique for keeping students focused on *outcomes*, and accountable for the time they spend—the idea is very much that they're always going to want to have something to report in their diary, so they have to ensure that every practice session moves them forwards in some way, rather than simply *passing time* playing stuff over and over.

This could easily be extended to lessons as well. The twist on the other techniques outlined in this chapter is that the student would be recognising and recording breakthroughs as they occur, rather than you being the chronicler.

Some students won't be very good at spotting achievements during the lesson itself, either because they don't know where to look, or because they get too busy actually playing. That's fine. They can be nudged.

For example, if they've finally just played a particular phrase in one breath—after months of otherwise needing to snatch a quick breath somewhere in the final two measures—but are then continuing on with the rest of the lesson like nothing happened, it's time to give them a poke:

> You know something...I don't think you've ever been able to play that section in one breath before.

And if they don't take the hint.

> Yes, now that I think about it—all in one breath—that's a **first**.

And if they're still looking at you like you're the final moments of an unusually complex Hercule Poirot reveal:

> I don't suppose you brought your breakthroughs diary with you today?

Why yes, yes I did. Why are you ask...wait! Ah! All in one breath! Do you have a pen? Did I *really?* I've *never* been able to do that. How about I put *this:* All...in...one...breath...the... really..long...run...June...22nd...Awesome!...

Awesome is right. Achievements *are* awesome. Students *love* them. And it turns out—as long as your attuned—they're *everywhere.*

The **Static Studio** has the *teacher* actively looking for reasons to give students *praise*
The **Dynamic Studio** has *students* actively looking for evidence of *achievements.*

Going the extra mile: the case for written reports

Music teachers often end up being among the most significant adults in a child's life; hardly surprising, given that we offer regular, extended and undivided one-on-one attention in a week which is otherwise normally filled with those same students being part of a crowd—a *shared desk* in a classroom, a *number on a back* at sports practice, a *member of a cast* in a dramatic production, *one of the Yellow belts* in a karate class. At their music lesson though it's just teacher and student, and in the course of a year of half-hour lessons, that means a lot of time together.

As a result, music teachers end up with insights into their students' various foibles and frustrations, qualities and quirks that even the child's parents might be unaware of; a music teacher will, for example, quickly get a very clear picture about *a student's willingness to take direction*, or their *persistence in the face of setbacks*, or their *capacity to perform under pressure*, or their *preparedness to work hard today for a result tomorrow* (or next month, or next year), or *how they respond to criticism*, or their *attention to detail*…or any one of dozens of other entirely transferable traits that will help or hinder that student in areas of their life that go well beyond music.

You can certainly share your insights by simply chatting with parents, but that's what all the other music studios in town are doing anyway; a central theme of this book is for your studio to provide value-added that parents simply can't get anywhere else. So, take a deep breath, and then ask yourself this:

How many studios do you know who provide *written reports* for their students, compiling the triumphs, concerns, insights and breakthroughs of the year that was into a single document for parents to read?

That might sound like a massive undertaking. Depending on how many students you have, it can be. But every minute you spend drafting these reports will be repaid in increased retention rates: where else in town will these parents find another music teacher whose dedication and professionalism is *this* evident, and who takes the time to understand their own students as well as you obviously understand yours?

> "...where else in town will these parents find another music teacher whose dedication and professionalism is *this* evident?"

Not just documentation for parents

If the idea of having to draft full length reports to every parent in the studio sounds like 30 hours you just don't have free, a powerful variation on this is for the reports you write to be designed for your *students* to read. In this case they don't need to be long or complex—in fact, simple and short is the only way they'll have any impact at all—but they still allow you to highlight the student's achievements and breakthroughs, but in digest form.

One clear and painless way to structure this is simply to present it as a *timeline*: the student's name at the top, and their milestones mapped against the months of the year underneath.

So when are you going to find time to assemble this? You don't need to find any time at all: keep the sheets handy during every lesson, simply add to them as the highlights emerge. Leave room for a sentence or two to summarise the entire year just before you officially hand it to them (ok, so you've got to find a few minutes for *that*), and you've got a report that is relatively painless to assemble, easy for a student to digest, while also providing telling evidence of just how much the student has achieved in the past 12 months.

You obviously shouldn't be waiting until you're writing reports to make students conscious of these breakthroughs, but seeing it reinforced in writing like that is a potent confirmation for both student and parent that you're not just *saying* these things. The key to credibility here is that the student has been given a consistent message across multiple mediums: they've been *told* that they (for example) play with some of the most engaging and wide-ranging dynamics of anyone in the studio; they've *received an award* for the very same; they've had the accolade publicly *dovetailed into an introduction* at a studio recital, and now—making it all seem capital "O" Official—it's been *chiselled into a written report.*

If this all seems too much...

I'm writing all this conscious of the fact that very few studios currently write reports for their students, or are likely to in the future.

You're in a minority already though to be considering it enough to have read this far; yours will be a rare studio indeed if you can summon the courage to make reports an official studio feature.

But a rare studio is exactly what any self-respecting music studio should be aiming to become.

 The **Static Studio** doesn't have time to give students written reports. The **Dynamic Studio** doesn't have time either, but finds it anyway.

What's next:

Creating evidence of progress for students is about dynamically cataloguing their *past*; in the next chapter we'll look at techniques for getting inside their heads to shape assumptions about the *future*—making it more likely that they'll be sharing that future with you.

Dynamic Soothsaying

Making the future a must-see show

Dynamic Soothsaying

WE HIGHLIGHTED IN THE INTRODUCTION THE problem of *perceived opportunity cost*—where students can be reluctant to stay with time-intensive and long-term commitments such as music lessons because of what they miss out on along the way.

The thing is though, opportunity cost can cut both ways, and—when lit from an appropriate angle—can actually become a powerful reason for students to stay. The idea is to vividly increase the perceived cost of leaving *your* activity; to ensure that parents and students have a compelling picture of the future they would forgo were they to pull the plug.

It leaves them with a warning that then has to weigh heavily on any decision they take about continuing lessons: leaving is not free. The cost is that their kids will miss out on *this* and *that* and *those things*.

Where will this compelling picture of the future come from? You're going to paint it for them. Parents and students need to understand what's possible in the short, medium and long term, and to be so excited about each of those phases that there's no way they'd want to miss out.

This chapter looks at the elements such a picture of the future can most usefully contain, and how best to communicate it.

Listening to the future

I'm not affiliated in any way, but one of the things that the Suzuki system does spectacularly well—and something that we could all learn from—is the immersive listening that students are expected to do well prior to the actually practice of a piece getting underway. It means that by the time a student is starting to actively work on a piece, they're already familiar with and understanding it at a level that just wouldn't be possible if they were starting it cold—I've written about this in both *Practiceopedia* and *The Practice Revolution*, and am still mystified as to why advance listening is not a feature in all teaching systems.

The pedagogical value of this strategy aside, there's a side-effect of listen-to-what's-coming-up that has enormous implications for retention rates: by getting students to listen to pieces that they *haven't played yet*, but *will at some point in the future*, you've got the student *visualising* that future. To listen repeatedly to a piece like that is inevitably to picture yourself playing it; any expert in goal setting, NLP or elite sports coaching will tell you that this is a huge step towards ensuring that this glimpse of the future will actually come about. In short, what your students listen to today is what their performances are likely to become tomorrow.

> "...leaving is not free. The cost is that their kids will miss out on *this* and *that* and *those things.*"

With recordings of so much of the repertoire legitimately available online as both audio and video, it's wilful negligence on any teacher's part for students not to have a playlist that reflects both what they're doing *now*, and what's going to be possible for them in the *future*. Talk to parents, explore how listening to that playlist could be hardwired into their week—in the car, while they do homework, during dinner, wherever—and then set up competitions that are focused on rewarding students for identifying what they're hearing. They won't necessarily be aware of the ulterior motive at work here, but in preparing for these competitions, the student inevitably and subconsciously establishes a whole series of repertoire targets for themselves.

This is then not just a playlist. This is a *timeline*. Cancelling lessons means erasing everything on that timeline that's after Right Now—for many parents and students, that can end up feeling like sabotage.

In the **Static Studio** students play pieces they've *been assigned.*
In the **Dynamic Studio**, student play pieces they've been *looking forward to for years.*

Living examples of what's next

Recordings are powerful, but an even more vivid way to have students visualising their future is to show them real, living examples of other students in the studio who are further down the path; the message is very much "this is what *you'll* be able to end up doing if you stick around."

> "...the message is very much "this is what you'll be able to end up doing if you stick around."

An ideal vehicle for this is studio recitals—you'll have the full range of your students there, from newest to most advanced—but what's going to be critical is how you *present* these students. It's not going to be enough to simply list the recital items and let the performances speak for themselves; parents need to be nudged towards the conclusions you want them to reach.

So as you're introducing a student, take a moment to provide some context that *highlights the timeline,* and helps every student in the room understand their place on it.

> "Some of you may remember our next performer from his very first recital, three years ago now, although you probably didn't *hear* it. He said afterwards that he was so nervous that he played as quietly as he could; that way nobody *would* hear him.
>
> None of those things are true now. Could you welcome to the stage, to show just what a difference three years and some great practice makes...Corey."

Applause. Oooh. Hasn't he *grown.* I *do* remember that performance, he was so scared. Shhh. It's starting...

...*wow!* Who knew Corey could play like *that?*

If you're in the audience, and your own child has ever been overcome by nerves, then this hasn't just been a performance, it's been an epiphany: just listen to *this* kid, he used to fret about performing too, look what's *possible.*

Not possible if the child leaves the studio, of course. You won't need to say that; parents will think it, and will think it all over again if their child ever talks about stopping lessons.

Corey's performance wasn't just a piece played. It was an immunization against other young, shy students leaving.

You can use the same tactic to project directly forwards—different student, different introduction, different emphasis:

> "Alicia has only been learning for 6 months, but she already has some of the most beautiful phrasing in the studio: just imagine one day what she'll be able to do with Chopin."

Everyone is imagining that now. But nobody is imagining it more than Alicia herself—she might not even know who or what *Chopin* is, but you can bet she'll be asking her parents in the car on the way home.

And so with a sentence—and a few strategic recording recommendations in the weeks after the recital—you might not only have boosted Alicia's confidence ahead of her very first recital, and got her parents thinking about a long term commitment to lessons, but established a life-long love of Chopin. Not a bad day at the office.

The **Static Studio** has beginner students who can't play what the advanced students can. The **Dynamic Studio** has beginner students who can't play what the advanced students can...*yet*...

Superpower wishlists

As many of your students will be able to tell you, one of the most motivating—and ubiquitous—features in computer games is the Talent Upgrade system. The idea is that the player is presented with a list of Superpowers to choose from, and then provided with a clear pathway to earn that particular upgrade.

So for their virtual orc-slaying barbarian, they might have to choose between a talent that has them permanently taking *10% less damage*, another that grants them *15 seconds of invisibility every half hour*, another still that allows them to *heal wounds*. Similarly, a virtual golfer might have to choose between an upgrade that allows them to *drive 5% further*, another that *increases the accuracy of their chip shots*, and still another that allows them to *replay one shot in every 9 holes, without penalty*.

Music students can be presented with similar upgrade possibilities in the form of a question:

Which of the following musical Superpowers would you like to have in a year's time?

To help their decision making you'd then supply them with a list of possible answers (carefully chosen, of course—see the chapter on Dynamic Autonomy ➡ 119) together with *examples* of other students who already have the superpower in question, to serve as inspiration. So, with the studio recital fresh in their minds, your list might cite the following possibilities:

Be able to publicly perform pieces **at sight**, like Alex did at the recital.

Be able to play pieces **by ear**, so that no music is necessary, like Simone opened the second half with.

Be able to **make up** your own pieces, like that awesome duet that Denise composed for Hugh and Kazuya.

Be able to play that insanely fast Brenner *Etude*, which you heard Angus nail as the final performance in the first half.

To know your **Major Scales** so well that you can survive the Spiralling Metronome Scales Challenge that you saw Katrina pull off just before the Awards segment of the recital.

To have enough repertoire under your fingers at one time to be able to give your **first 20 minute solo recital program,** like we heard Hassan do earlier this year.

To have uploaded recordings to YouTube of **30 different pieces in 30 weeks.** (Beating Klaus's 25 pieces in 25 weeks), as proof of mastering *speed-learning* pieces.

This is an entirely different way of working—the student isn't just gearing up for Yet Another Recital, but is now committing to working towards a specific superpower in the future.

And as game developers know only too well, the very fact that they're so focused on that future then makes it much more likely that they'll be sharing it with you—to earn the upgrade, you have to stay on the path.

 The **Static Studio** *teaches* students how to play. The **Dynamic Studio** has students *working towards* new abilities.

Paddling in the shallow end of the future

All the techniques in this chapter so far have essentially been about visualization, as you get students to *vividly imagine*, and then *become excited by*, and then *commit to realizing* possibilities in their musical future. You can start to solidify these projections by letting them actually paddle in the shallow end of that future, right now.

You might, for example, have an early intermediate piano student who has just discovered Rachmaninoff after watching both *Shine* and a documentary on the Van Cliburn piano competition, and is now fascinated by the infamous 3rd Concerto. As someone who is still years away from coping with even the easiest of the Rachmaninoff *Preludes*, this student won't have anywhere near the technical skills needed to cope with that concerto yet (99.99% of piano students *never* end up with skills sufficient to tame that work) but even a relative beginner could cope with the very first page or so, with it's slow, single line melody.

Where's the harm in letting the student learn that much, while they then daydream about the rest? What's to be lost by then highlighting that before they could learn the rest of *that* enormous work, they'd need to do *this* slightly less imposing one, and before *that*, *this* that's easier still, and before that *this*…with a trail of prerequisites that leads right back to the piece they're starting *this very week?*

It's all about them seeing their lessons as a *chain*, where the work they do today demonstrably links to extraordinary possibilities in the future. They might not follow that chain all the way to Rach 3, (or whatever the equivalent Everest piece is for the instrument you teach), but they will follow it much further than if the future hadn't been presented as a carrot on the stick—or perhaps more accurately, as a trail of breadcrumbs.

This trail is not reproducible, something to clone and then issue to every student. It's dynamic. Created just for *this* student, like a personalised time machine.

It's only human nature then to want to take the trip.

 The **Static Studio** helps students *focus* on the piece that's *coming up next*.
The **Dynamic Studio** gets students *daydreaming* about possibilities in their *distant future*.

Using reports to set up the future

We looked in the Dynamic Scoreboards chapter (➡162) at the case for teachers actually issuing written reports for their students, primarily as a vehicle for giving students a compelling and clear sense of progress. Studio reports obviously can shed plenty of light on the Year That Was, but they do some of their best work when they lay expectations for what's Yet To Come.

So if the first part of a report highlights that Timothy's difficulty with sightreading is actually doubling the amount of practice he needs to do to learn new pieces, then it makes sense for Part 2 of the report to be an outline of what you're planning to do to turn this problem around: *Here's what we'll do immediately. Here's what we'll transition to in a couple of months. And here's the deep end I'll be throwing him into in a year from now, when his sightreading powers are transformed.*

> "...the very fact that you're talking about what will be happening a *year from now* helps parents adopt a longer term view to lessons"

Detailing your thinking like this achieves a number of things, all of them good for student retention:

First of all, it reminds parents that there's nothing in your teaching which is arbitrary; that *today's* lessons are crafted based on what you observed *yesterday*, and what you plan for *tomorrow* is very much based on what you've seen *today*, and are approaching lessons not just with enthusiasm, but genuine strategy.

Secondly, it helps soften the impact of any concerns you might have listed in the main body of the report, by leaving parents with the reassurance that these issues—while worth highlighting—are *fixable*, and *here's what we're going to do about it.*

And thirdly—and most usefully— it *extends the horizon*: the very fact that you're talking about what will be happening a *year from now* helps parents adopt a longer term view to lessons, and sends the message that you're certainly not imagining this student leaving any time soon. In so doing, you've just made the lesson-ending conversation harder for them to initiate, both because you'd obviously be shocked by any withdrawal (you were, after all, outlining detailed plans for the next twelve months), and because it's not just the *present* that they'd be cancelling: they'd be shutting down all these *future plans* as well.

And that, right there, is where the report is so potent as a force for student retention. It highlights *the future possibilities forgone were the student to leave*, and in so doing adds a price tag to stopping lessons that many parents will find too steep.

The **Static Studio** *answers questions* about the past when parents ask how their child is progressing. The **Dynamic Studio** *proactively provides* assessments and outlines *plans for the future.*

Hyping distant events

One of the hallmarks of the Dynamic Studio is the capacity to create memorable events that transcend the same-old that is the endless parade of Static Studio Recitals. If you can get students looking forward to your event enough, then the mere fact that it's *coming up* can become a potent reason for otherwise outgoing students to rethink—or at least defer—their exit.

The self-talk you're hoping for is a sentence that begins with "I should at least stick it out until…", but if all you've got coming up in the next twelve months are two more of the same old studio recitals that you've always held in the past, then there's no compelling reason for a student to even begin that sentence in the first place. Now is as good a time to quit as any.

But if your studio will be hosting a Short Film Festival early next year, at which students in the studio will be providing all the background music, and which will be the subject of a documentary for a local news channel, then you've just added to the cost of leaving. The student is still free to leave, but they'd miss out on *this*, and it promises to be tremendous fun.

And of course, as a Dynamic Studio, that event would be one of several, as your calendar also proudly highlights the *Sightreading Olympiad* and a *conducting camp* and an *excursion to the GigaBlast SoundEffects Studio* and the *launch of the studio magazine…*

It's the reason that theatre and opera companies always flag productions that open *next* year in printed programs from *this* year. The message to subscribers? Stick around. The future looks unusually exciting; you don't want to miss a second.

 The **Static Studio** *schedules* regular studio recitals that students can *work towards*.
The **Dynamic Studio** *hypes* landmark events that students can *look forward to*.

What's next:

No matter how exciting the future might seem, if students aren't made to feel special in the present, then lessons almost certainly won't get that far. There's more to affirmation though than mere positive reinforcement: the next chapter looks at how to dial this element of your teaching way, way up.

Dynamic Affirmations

The art of making students feel special

Dynamic Affirmations

TEACHING MUSIC WOULD BE VERY EASY, save for one inconvenient reality: our teaching schedules are not actually populated with *music students*; they're populated with *people*.

The distinction is important: it's a differentiation between an ideal and a reality. Music students—of the sort that much of our pedagogy training prepares us for—are an abstraction, defined in terms of *educational outcomes* and *recontextualized process-based competencies* and *enhanced meaning-centered paradigms* and other nonsense that has no practical meaning whatsoever when you have an eight-year-old human being in front of you who would much rather tell you about their new puppy than listen to you talk about key signatures.

There's no way to handle what comes next for this student with an "ology" or an "ism", or an appeal to some sort of platonic form of what a beginner music student *ought* or *ought not* be. You've never taught anybody quite like her before, nor will you again—including the version of her that you see in her very next lesson, when she's a week older, and stuff has happened, and *something* about her will be different. Which means the instructions can't be found in anything so static as a *book*, including this one.

Because the clients who walk through our studio doors are people, and not textbook archetypes, they therefore bring with them all the attendant frailties and needs that we should be expecting from any other human being.

And of all these needs, none is as fundamental—or collides with the Static Studio so badly—as the need to feel *special*.

For the Dynamic Studio—the studio that by definition is student centred, and continuously reinvents itself in orbit around that principle—*this* is a need that we *have* to continuously meet.

Obviously none of us actually treat our students like archetypes or numbers; we know it's important to differentiate curriculum, and be personable and friendly, and interested, and whatever.

But remember, the Dynamic Studio is not just about eliminating the bad, or adding the new. It's about also taking good things that *do* exist and dialling them way, way up.

> "...of all these needs, none is as fundamental—or collides with the Static Studio so badly—as the need to feel *special*."

This chapter looks at doing exactly that, with the specific goal of having every student you teach feeling that they're the student you think about and look forward to teaching the most, and are proudest to show off to *other* parents and students.

This is not about cheap self-esteem boosting tricks. To give the illusion of paying this sort of close attention to your students, *you're going to actually have to pay close attention to your students.* As we'll see, that produces a cascade of positive effects not just for the student and for yourself, but for the entire studio.

So how can you make your students feel special? Let us count the ways.

Being excited about their extramusical talents

It's easier to make students feel special if you're able to work directly with those unique qualities that genuinely *do* make them special. The key here for the Dynamic Studio is that many of those qualities will have nothing to do with music.

When a student tells you that they're the age-group chess champion for their district, or that they made the dress they're wearing, no music teacher is going to be callous enough to say "that's nice" and move straight on, but what's key here is not how you react at the time. It's going to be what systems you have in place to ensure that this information *resurfaces* in the future.

Think about it from your student's point of view. It's one thing for them to have told you about their own achievements, and then have you react positively, but it is particularly delicious for you to then *bring up* those achievements weeks later in conversation with someone else, like you're a proud grandmother.

> **"...if it's important enough to the student for them to be telling you about it in the first place, it's important enough to make a note of."**

Oh *stop* it, they'll protest. You're *embarrassing* me. No you're not. You're making their day. And you're proving you were paying attention, way back whenever, and that your interest in them goes beyond that obligated by the fact that they're your student.

This is not as easy as it sounds though. With lots of students in the studio, most of whom are volunteering trivia about themselves with abandon during lessons, we get inundated with information like this, and it's very easy to lose track. The guideline for the Dynamic Studio is a simple one: whether it seems like trivia or not, if it's important enough to the student for them to be telling you about it in the first place, it's important enough to make a note of.

And so, while Static Studios will often keep notes about the musical development of their students, a Dynamic Studio will have space set aside for What This Student Is Proud Of.

It means then that at the next studio recital—it could be six months after you were first told about your chess player and dressmaker—instead of introducing *pieces*, you can introduce your *students*:

> "Next up, playing the famous Donati *Largo*, is Dean Wellsmore. He might *seem* like a nice guy, but you don't want to sit down across a chessboard from him—he will crush you like a grape... and you'll have no idea how he did it. Age group district chess champion this year, and an excellent violin student too, could you please welcome Dean."

Huge smiles from Dean. Huge smiles from his parents. *My teacher remembered!*

You did...because you consulted the notes in the week leading up to the recital itself. Dean doesn't need to know that.

What's important here is then not whether he plays well that afternoon. It's that he's walking taller because you obviously paid attention to something he said to you in passing *months* ago.

And straight after Dean? Your notes have reminded you that this next student *makes her own clothes*, so:

> "You might think Helen is looking particularly sharp today, in a dress that should be hanging up in Rodeo Drive...but she *made* it, together with the dress of her duet partner. Tonight you should give her your full attention; in the future though, you may just want to give her your measurements. Ladies and Gentlemen—Helen Jackson."

Enter Helen. All eyes are on the dress. She's beaming.

None of this has anything to do with music. It has everything to do with a significant adult in the student's life making them feel *important*. It costs you nothing except the willingness to pay attention when students have news to share (which Static Studios will also do), and then *being organised enough to note the details* (which a Static Studio is less likely to do), and then to be prepared to *find occasions to spread the pride*—whether it's in a Big Event such as a studio recital, or simply bringing up the student's talent from time-to-time in lessons.

Of course, not all students will be as forthcoming about their own achievements, which can leave you with gaps in these most important of notes. However the student is only one of many possible sources; from the student's point of view, the only thing even better than highlighting something they've told you is highlighting something they *never* told you, but that you've found out from parents, or another teacher, or a sibling. This combines the thrill of being spotlit with the mystery of "but how did my *music teacher* know?"

For that reason, the Dynamic Studio is regularly prodding the family of their students—the message is very clearly "keep me informed." If the student wins a ribbon, appears in the paper, is the lead in the school play, can ride a horse, appeared as an extra in a commercial, was voted class captain, got their 25 metres breaststroke certificate, can make pasta from scratch or knows how to tell time just by looking at the sun, then you want to know...so you can *celebrate* it.

Bragging on behalf of your students. It's a great part of the job. But how many of your students, right now, have talents you're not sure of, can't remember, or never knew about in the first place?

The **Static Studio** will patiently *listen* when students talk about their other talents. The **Dynamic Studio** *seeks out, files away* and *reuses* the information.

Personalised Rewards

In an age that tailors everything to the individual—from search engine results that evolve based on your browsing history to custom-fit jeans—it's harder than it used to be to impress students with a generic, everybody-gets-one certificate for their efforts.

Creating awards that resonate is a challenge for any studio, but is a priority for the Dynamic Studio: as we'll see elsewhere in the book, there's just too much that depends on students being given regular and meaningful evidence of their own progress.

One tactic is to join the great age of personalization, and create rewards that are tailored specifically for the student.

The trick is to look for the intersection between a *trait* unique to the student and whatever the *breakthrough itself* was. So if you have a student who is forever driving their parents nuts by insisting on wearing a baseball cap into lessons, but who recently gave a memorably arresting first performance of a piece they had always feared was impossible, then you *could* put a sticker in an Achievements Book...

> "...creating awards the resonate is a challenge for any studio, but is a *priority* for the Dynamic Studio."

...or you could create a unique reward he'll look back fondly on for years to come. Find a company that will do the lettering, and then get a *commemorative baseball cap* for him:

I defeated the Kwiatowski Sonata!

It's very much an in-joke—only you and the student will understand just why a *baseball cap* is the perfect gift, or will even know what the *Kwiatowski Sonata* is in the first place. So he'll probably never wear it out. But he'll almost certainly wear it to lessons, and this time his parents will be smiling too.

And if you want to take it further, and get this student thinking about the future—a tactic we looked at in the previous chapter (➡ 167)—then print a *second* hat, with the name of an even tougher piece on it. Show it to him, but don't give it to him... yet. If he's up to the challenge, it's his as soon as he performs the piece.

The point in each case wasn't the hat, it was that the hat was *just right* for this student—a different student would have triggered a completely different reward. So if you have a student who is always complaining about how cold your studio is (there's always one), then their gift is likewise a no-brainer. The only question is what the hot water bottle should have written on it: that would be determined by whatever their achievement was. Again, it's the intersection between a *trait* unique to the student, and whatever their *breakthrough* was.

What's special about these rewards is that they're not inter-changeable—*those* items with *those* words written on them couldn't possibly be for anybody else in the studio apart from the students they were intended for. The recipients will think you must have gone out of your way to create something especially for them (you did!); the result is not then a certificate to put on the fridge for a week and then *discard*, but an award they'll treasure and *keep*.

The **Static Studio** thinks a certificate will do, because it's the thought that counts. The **Dynamic Studio** knows that it actually *is* the thought that counts, which is why a certificate won't do.

Being aware of—and taking delight in—their foibles and quirks.

One of the great challenges for any studio—Static or Dynamic— is handling students with personality traits or patterns of behaviour that are actively at odds with a productive lesson.

You'll think straight away of plenty of examples of your own, but I had a student once who spoke so fast and so much that Robin Williams would have told her to shift it down a notch. Given also that most of what she talked about had nothing whatsoever to do with whatever it was we were supposed to be doing (and after a couple of minutes, who could even remember what *that* was?), the temptation was to tell her to shut up so we could actually get something done.

Much more effective, I discovered by accident, was *not* to interrupt her; to let the five minute rant run its course, and wait until she needed to inhale, at which point I was able to shoehorn a question of my own into the monologue:

"What" I asked during the respite "on *earth* are you talking about?"

At which point she grinned and admitted that she had no idea.

"So…this talking—at a bazillion miles an hour—with no idea what's coming out your mouth, does that happen a lot?"

All the time. Wanna hear more?

"Um. No. But I could hear some Chopin. As long as you promise to play the middle section slower than you rant. You're going to take someone's eye out if you're not careful."

From that lesson on, her *ranting speed* became not a reason for annoyance, but an unofficial unit of measurement for tempo for us both: 0.5 of how fast she talked was a good, brisk allegro. 0.8 is already prestissimo. 1.0 would simply trigger an instant technical catastrophe at the piano, and quite probably a fire.

Months later, at a masterclass, as another student was playing something *much* too fast, I leant across to her and whispered "Hmmm. 0.9. I think someone should call an ambulance".

She didn't say anything in reply, but there was a huge smile. There was no other student in the room who would have understood what I had just said; this was a private moment that quietly communicated to her something very simple:

"I enjoy working with you."

Which is absolutely true. I did enjoy working with her—it was an energising, unpredictable and thoroughly rewarding way to spend half an hour each week.

Of course we didn't always get as much done as I would have liked, and this is a student I easily could have been frustrated with. But as a teacher, the greatest worry is not if a student like that won't stop talking. It's if they *do*. Her motormouth was a huge part of who she was; had I tried to shut it down, or obviously found it irritating, then we really shouldn't be spending time together.

What was particularly interesting about this case is that I found out from her parents that her school reports were filled with teachers venting about her lack of self-control; but because I cut her some slack occasionally, and took genuine delight in her circumlocutorially loquastic quirks, my approval was *important* to her—and so if I ever did need her to shut up and listen, she would, in a way that she would for few other people. She had a license to rant in my studio; in return, I had a license for her full attention.

Think about your students for a moment. Think particularly about their foibles; the students who are *always late*, the students who keep *mixing up their left hand with their right*, the students who insist on playing even their *mezzo-fortes* as though the Four Horsemen of the Apocalypse were drunk and disorderly in a saucepan factory—all things that could well drive any teacher crazy.

Now think: how can you find it within yourself to actually take delight in these quirks? How can you laugh about it with your students, and help them to laugh at the quirk with you? How can you find quiet moments to confirm that you love working with them not just in spite of these shortcomings, but —oddly enough—*because* of them?

Don't confuse this with not wanting to gently moderate their behaviour. The Dynamic Studio would still have a responsibility to tone down those mezzo-fortes before concert day. But if that means that as a running gag you rewrite *all* dynamics for that student—replacing mfs with ps, and ps with pppppps—to get the desired outcome, then so be it. If other students see the markings on the score and ask what on earth is going on, you don't need to explain—just exchange glances with your mezzo-forte challenged student and note the big grin.

"This was a private moment that quietly communicated to her something very simple: "*I enjoy working with you.*""

(Nothing says "I'm not planning on leaving this studio any time soon" quite like regular big grins. If I ever were to write a Readers Digest condensed one-sentence version of this book, it would say that.)

The **Static Studio** *tolerates* and *moderates* the quirks of their students. The **Dynamic Studio** *delights* in them, and wouldn't have their student any other way.

Being excited about their *musical* strengths

When students have their lessons, the list of criticisms they are subject to can seem dauntingly long: we ask them to be mindful of (please) intonation, phrasing, posture, dynamics and articulation; also watch out for projection, unity, contrast, fingering and tone production, tempo choice, tempo control, rubato, ornamentation, melodic line integrity...

> "...students who think they're nothing special have no special reason to stay."

...the fact that this list is so extensive can come in very handy though: with so many parameters to choose from, *it should be possible to find at least one to highlight as being a genuine strength*, and then make a rallying point for the student's entire musical self-image.

So you might have one student who has a spectacular dynamic range, and excellent tone right across that spectrum. Make sure they know that this is both unusual, and a Very Good Thing. You're not making that up—it *is* unusual and a Very Good Thing.

What then to do with this information? Highlight it as a special ability whenever they're with other students. Point it out to their parents. Use the student as a best-practice example on this issue in the studio newsletter or website. Talk about it again before they perform at studio recitals. Have them showcase selected passages in studio workshops and masterclasses. Upload a video of a performance to your YouTube channel (➡ 260)

An excellent student, yes? Not at all. Spectacular dynamic range, certainly, but this particular student might have no sight-reading skills, nor be able to maintain a constant tempo, and produce fingering that look like it escaped from a phone book—

all things that will have to be addressed in lessons at some stage. But those potentially discouraging limitations are not how they'll be defining themselves; your care not just to talk up but give *flagship status* to what they *are* good at will ensure that they are looking forward to showing what they can do in every lesson and performance opportunity.

But of course, you know this, yes? Which means that every student on your schedule—*all of them*—are aware of what they do better than almost anybody else?

If it's possible you've missed a few, then there's still work to be done. Students who think they're nothing special have no special reason to stay. The Dynamic Studio can't afford to relax on this critical issue until every student has a legitimate reason to be proud.

Mapping the Ideal Student

Once you're clear on what special quality each student brings to their lessons, a compelling way to highlight these various traits to the whole studio is to create an annual portrait of the Ideal Student; a montage assembled from the best of what each student offers.

So, for example, the perfect student might have...

...the *posture* of **Alex**; the *patience* of **Simone**; the *scales and technical work mastery* of **Sachin**; the *sense of space between phrases* of **Dalia**; the *unfailing punctuality* of **Preston**; the *sense of humour* of **Leota**; the *precise rhythmic delivery* of **Pete**; the *sightreading skills* of **Gerardo**; the *singing melodic lines* of **Breanna**; the *infectious cheerfulness* of **Damon**; the *intonation* of **Doris**; the *sparkling passagework* of **Portia**...

...and so on, until every student in the studio has been referenced once, for an attribute that no other student is listed for.

Turn it into a poster, update it at the end of each year. The unveiling of each year's new list will be keenly anticipated by the students, and is worthy of a spotlight moment at any big studio recital or official dinner you might have—everyone will be wondering just where they fit into this Ideal Student jigsaw puzzle.

You don't have to be drawn on the details, but you can let everyone know that there were actually many, many categories that most students could have been listed in—that way, they'll understand that the trait you've highlighted is not the only thing you value about them. So while you might have cited *the posture of Alex*, it's important that everyone knows that there are other students in the studio whose posture is excellent; it's similarly important that Alex knows that there are other categories he would have been eligible for. (again, it's important not to be specific if pushed; omissions will be keenly felt)

> "...it's not just a compendium of reasons for your students to be proud—it's also an A-Z of the values your studio holds as being important."

Otherwise though, this list is not just a compendium of reasons for your students to be proud—it's also an A-Z of the values your studio holds as being important, and a potent reminder to all parents as to just how multi-dimensional your expectations actually are.

The **Static Studio** gives *positive reinforcement*.
The **Dynamic Studio** celebrates *unique student attributes*, and celebrates *hard*.

Assigning students roles

This book has talked a lot about the importance of *diversity* to the Dynamic Studio; part of the logic underpinning this is that a studio with a breadth of offerings is providing additional reasons for students to stay—it's the reason that theme parks don't just have one ride.

But the other reason is that all these additional options provides the potential for additional *connections*. The more links a student has to your studio, the more ties they actually have to cut to leave, and therefore the more painful leaving actually becomes. So a student who is not only having weekly lessons, but also has a regular duet partner in your studio Ensemble Program, and is one of your Team Green of improvisers in your Making It Up On The Spot club will have three different threads that they have to cut if they were to leave. It's a much, much tougher call for them to make than it is for a student who simply has a weekly lesson.

Giving students a *role* in the studio creates yet another such thread but goes one better: the fact that you've trusted them with the responsibility of a role helps them to feel special too.

So what could these roles be? It's most effective—and will be most valued by the student—if they're determined not by some sort of arbitrary roster-wheel, but based directly on the student's strengths. So if you have a student who has just been named in the state squad for debating, then that's your MC for the next studio recital. A student whose artwork caught your eye in the local school magazine (the Dynamic Studio always reads these...you never know when or which of your students will be highlighted) might be tasked with creating the image for the poster for your upcoming studio recital. Another student who has been talking non-stop about the camera she got for her birthday would be put in charge of photos of the event. Cakes would be done by the student who surprised you on your birthday with a cake he made himself. The studio website might be maintained by a student who is also trying to get established as a web designer (your very public thanks and endorsement at the studio recital might just get them some of their very first clients).

The jobs don't need to be essential. They just need to *seem* essential to the students. If that means manufacturing some responsibilities based on some unusual talents, then so be it—so if you have a student who is into electronics kits, instead of her making yet another doorbell, commission a *metronome* for the studio.

If you pay attention, it should be possible to find a role for every student in the studio. With all these threads being established and then worked, your studio isn't just being active; it's being *woven*.

 Leaving a **Static Studio** means ending *lessons*. Leaving a **Dynamic Studio** means breaking *ties*.

Enjoying lesson time without having to get things done

With only limited lesson time available, teachers can feel significant pressure to extract as much as possible from every second—which means keeping the Corrections Per Minute (CPM) count as high as possible.

That sounds logical enough—in a 19th Century factory owner kind of way—but there's more than productivity at play here. Lessons with relentlessly high CPM might appear more productive, but like any factory floor, the incessant expectations often comes with a drop in morale.

There's an entire chapter in this book devoted to making your studio more fun (➡ 209), but none of that is going to be possible unless you can give yourself permission not to regard *downtime* as *wasted* time.

In a world which demands *more* and *now* and *faster*, this can be an extraordinarily tough shift in thinking to make.

But that 10 minutes you "lost" while the student enthuses about their new hamster, or wants to show you the ending they made up for their Bach Minuet (see! Chopsticks fits right in! Who knew?), or showing you their medal from today's cross-country event, or putting forward their theory about how violins would sound better if they were made from carbon fibre rather than wood...all these and many, many more "timewasters" like them will be more than made up for by the increase in the strength of the connection between you and the student.

> "...like any factory floor, the incessant expectations often comes with a drop in morale"

The message students will take away is that you value spending time with them in a way that transcends the mundane busyness of Helping Them To Play Better. It means that when the time comes for you to give feedback that they *really* need to hear, the very strength of the relationship will lend your words urgency, and guarantee their attention.

This idea is not without precedent. Think tacking in the breeze. Or a professional racing driver braking early for corners so they can lap quickly. Or siestas that interrupt otherwise frenetic Mexican business days. Or 19th Century master composers and poets who lose hours each day going for walks.

Forwards, with everything you've got is great advice for a finalist in the 100m at the Olympic games. But if *forwards* is the only direction available to your music students, and *with everything you've got* is the only speed you'll accept, then unless your studio consists entirely of Type-A personalities with serious music ambitions, you have no right to complain when they leave.

 The **Static Studio** has students running in their lanes, and running hard. The **Dynamic Studio's** students are known to have been seen walking. Or skipping. Or dancing. Or just *sitting*.

Overheard Praise

Most music teachers are well aware of the power of positive reinforcement, but tossing praise about like it's wedding confetti can lead to students becoming desensitised to superlatives of any kind. Of *course* I'm clever and special and have done excellent work and you're so proud and my phrasing is beautiful; you tell me every week, and so did my last music teacher.

Whatever.

But not all praise is equal, nor so readily dismissible. If you've ever been in the right place at the right time to accidentally overhear someone saying nice things about you—when it was

clear that they didn't realise you were party to the conversation—
then you'll know exactly what I mean:

There is no more credible, effective or adhesive praise than
that which was never intended to be heard.

Which is exactly why you should be staying alert for opportunities to deliver such overheard praise of your own.

Now before the protests start, I know it sounds horribly
Machiavellian to set up overheard praise for such ends, but really
all you're doing is:

1) **choosing** something positive that you sincerely want the
student to know that you believe of them, and then

2) **delivering** that message in a way that they cannot forget
easily.

You might be contriving the medium, your motives might
be opaque, but you're sincere about the message; the overheard
praise is simply a (highly effective) vehicle for communicating
something that you would have them know anyway.

So how do you engineer this? Once you're actively looking
for opportunities, you'll be surprised by how often they present
themselves. Lets look at four of the easiest to seize:

Option 1: The studio recital

These are fertile ecosystems for overheard praise, because you have
all your students in one space, with dozens of simultaneous conversations taking place as students mill about before and after the
main event. It's a day when you'll be talking to a *lot* of people, and
it's entirely reasonable for bystanders to assume that you're not necessarily aware of who is in earshot as you're making your comments.

Let's imagine then that it's the interval during once such
recital, and you're circulating in the foyer, chatting to parents and
students about performances that just took place in the first half.

You spot a student who is not talking to you, but standing with their back to you within dead-cat-swing distance, deep in conversation with someone else. Perfect. They won't be actively listening to what you're talking about, but when you start to talk about *them*, cocktail-party syndrome will kick in; their name will leap out from the background chatter, and they *will* hear what you're about to say. In fact, until you've finished talking about them, they probably won't hear anything else.

The whole thing works like this:

"I've been delighted with the first half" you can say "But there's a performance you should be really watching out for in the second half: the girl is called Amelia, she's playing a Schubert Sonata…"

Kazam. The targeted student hasn't turned around, but cocktail-party syndrome has tapped her on the shoulder, as "Girl called Amelia playing a Schubert Sonata" has cut through the babel like a dog whistle; Amelia is still nominally a participant in her original conversation, but she's really not listening to that any more. Ooooh! Girl called Amelia playing a Schubert Sonata! That's me! Where's my teacher going with this?…

> "…if you're going to be praising students, it might as well be for something they're *actually good at*, and it might as well *stick*."

"…She plays with great control, but what you really want to listen out for is her phrasing—it's beautifully shaped, and she has some truly original ideas. I know you've got a great ear for stuff like this, and I think when you hear Amelia, you'll agree there's a really interesting musical mind at work there…maybe you two should do a duet together one day."

Truly original ideas. Interesting musical mind at work. You should listen out for her phrasing. The only thing Amelia is thinking now is "don't stop!". But you can stop now; this payload has already been successfully delivered.

It took just twenty seconds, but three very positive—and enduring—changes have just come out of this encounter:

> 1) Amelia now knows that you value her as a student—enough to recommend her(!) to another student(!!) as an example of excellence(!!!).

> 2) She will be pushing especially hard in her upcoming performance to produce creative and compelling phrasing, and will do so with the confidence of someone who knows they're believed in.

> 3) The chances of Amelia quitting any time soon have likely just evaporated.

Have you manipulated Amelia? A little, perhaps, in that your unawareness of her presence was feigned. But you haven't really been disingenuous as this all sounds: you've only highlighted aspects of her playing that were genuinely worth praising in the first place. This would be an important thing to do for Amelia even if it had nothing to do whatsoever with retention rates; if you're going to be praising students, it might as well be for something they're *actually good at*, and it might as well *stick*.

So this is not deception so much as steering her thinking in a direction that brings out her best. Hard to fault that.

Option 2: The parent aside

Not every overheard-praise moment depends on having a mass gathering of your entire studio. This second option is a technique you can use at the lesson itself, and needs no more than the student and at least one of their parents.

For this to work, you need to ask the student if they would mind waiting just outside the door, as you want to be able to talk privately to the parent. Students are normally cheshire-cat curious to know what is being said about them, so you can be certain that right outside the door is exactly where they'll be. Perfect.

All you need to do now is to position yourself with your back to the (pushed to, but not entirely closed) door when you talk, and project your voice just a little…the student should hear every word:

"Listen, I just wanted to give you a heads up about something I've noticed with Daniel recently"

If Daniel's ear is not on the door after hearing that, then he's just not human. Am I in trouble? What could be so important that I need to be *banished* while the news is given?

But you're not running this exercise to relay concerns:

"I don't think I've ever seen a student improve their scales so quickly as Dan has in the past month—I was absolutely blown away by the test we had last lesson. I don't want him to know, but I'm actually looking at him for a special award at the end of the year; just making sure that you are able to keep the date of the presentation evening free."

Of course, let me check my calendar, we'd love to be there.

Meanwhile, on the other side of the door, Daniel will be beside himself. Special award? Actually, hold that…a *secret* special award? My scales are awesome?

Apart from the fact that Daniel's scales practice is now likely to double, we now have a student who knows he's valued by you—not in a vague "you're great" meaningless way, but because of specifics that reflect his *actual strengths*. With the awards ceremony slated for "the end of the year", you've also provided him with a powerful reason to stick around until at least then (see also hyping future landmarks ➡ 177).

If Daniel now quits despite all *that*, then he was never a student that you were going to be able to keep in the first place—so be it. But it wasn't for lack of intervention on your part.

Option 3: Passed on praise

If you ever find yourself raving to your own family about how wonderful one of your students is, consider also making a quick call to that student's family to share your enthusiasm. Parents love to hear their child's name and deserved superlatives in the same sentence, and you can be sure that they'll pass on what was said…at which point this becomes a form of overheard praise. Students need to *know they're valued*, and are happiest when they're *doing well:* your phone call has just established powerful evidence of both—much more so than if you had merely put a sticker on a book.

A variation on this is to write a note addressed to the parents, or shoot them an email—ostensibly for their eyes only, but once they read the good news inside, you know they'll be passing it on. Again, the fact that you're praising to a *third party* lends credibility to the message: you must be really serious about the content if you're going to the trouble to notify parents.

You *are* serious about the content. You'd love to have the student believe the message of themselves, and for them to know that you believe it of them too; it's all about your lessons obviously causing the student to walk a little taller. It's a big call for a parent to wind that up: why shut down something that's obviously going so well, and is such a source of pride for their child?

Option 4: Unexpected Guest Stars

Another variable that can dramatically ramp up the impact of overheard praise is the question of *who* you were relaying that praise to, and *how significant* that person is to the student.

If, for example, the student has a *favourite school teacher* or *sports coach* that they talk about a lot, or a *big sister* who has moved interstate, and only occasionally visits now, then it's worth inviting these special people to one of your studio recitals. Make sure your student notices their unexpected guests in the audience before the concert starts…and then take the time to enthuse publicly about your student in the introduction to their performance. You don't need to acknowledge the guests as you do this—in fact, it's better that you conduct yourself as if you had completely forgotten they were there. The impression should be that these are the things you would have been saying anyway.

This is particularly potent overheard praise, although it's a reversal of how things normally work: it's not the student who's "overhearing" it, but an assembly of many of the people the student would most want to shine in front of. Thanks to the fact that you were alert to the opportunity, your student has just done exactly that; this has been a memorable day for them…and it was your music lessons that made it all possible.

The **Static Studio** does their best work *one-on-one*, when the student has their full attention.
The **Dynamic Studio** does some of their best work when the student *doesn't even think they're in the frame.*

Celebrating their birthday

It would be a stone-hearted teacher indeed who wouldn't make a fuss about a student's birthday...as long as they *know*. And that knowledge is the key here: it's one thing to smile and say "happy birthday" in response to a student who has just told you that Sunday was the Big Day; it's another thing entirely for them to have got a text or a card from you *on* that Sunday, unprompted.

The problem here is not one of *intent*, it's one of *triggering*. 50 students means 50 birthdays to keep track of, but that's not so hard if you've entered them into whatever calendar program you use. Set it to notify you two weeks in advance—this allows for the "hey, isn't it someone's birthday next week?" opener at the lesson, and then again on or just before the day so you can send your message.

It's a small thing. Actually, scrap that—it's a *huge* thing. Birthdays and kids, they want the whole world to know, and you're actually a surprisingly big part of that whole world.

The **Static Studio** *congratulates* students in response to *being told* it's their birthday. The **Dynamic Studio** *delights* students by not needing to be told in the first place.

Making them famous

Your student's excellent result in the recent practice competition is probably not going to be the lead story on CNN, but you can feature their photo in your studio newsletter or website, followed by the kind of story that would normally only appear for someone who *is* famous.

So you might interview your student, and quote some of their responses. You might include a **profile**—a brief bio, much as you might see for a movie or sporting celebrity. You might include **comments** and **quotes** from people who know them— parents, school teachers, friends—talking briefly about *how hard they work*, or *how focused they are*, or *what a good soccer player they are*. Nothing too personal, or that would breach any sort of confidentiality considerations, just affirmations of some positive personality traits.

You might include their answers to a 10 questions type **personal trivia quiz**—the sort that celebrity magazines churn out: their *least favourite food*, what they would *spend their last $10 on*, would they ever consider *bungee jumping*, would they rather have a pet *penguin* or a pet *zebra*—stupid questions like that, to which the answers would only ever be interesting if the person were famous somehow (therefore they *must* be!)

You could produce a poster for the studio announcing the Practice Champion of Summer with their name and photo both set large. Or if the competition were a significant annual event, you may want to have their name inscribed on a studio honour board (➡ 245).

And when the end of year recital rolls around—and the student thinks you've forgotten all about it—resurrect their triumph one more time:

> ...and of course, this summer we had a brand new Practice Champion, with Taylor Dennett racking up more than a dozen practice Achievements to take the prize. We might just give Taylor one more round of applause...

This was just one competition triumph, and already Taylor has been the subject of a studio newsletter profile, a celebrity quiz, a poster, a permanent inscription on the studio honour board, and a special mention in your end-of-year wrap...it's not just Taylor who's going to be excited by this. Plenty of other students will be wishing it were them—and quietly looking for opportunities where it could be. (That's fine. You'll be creating loads of such opportunities...the chapter on Dynamic Rewards ➡229) is packed with possibilities for exactly this.).

And of course watching from the sideline will be parents, impressed by the trouble you're prepared to go to to celebrate student successes...which other music teachers in town would be prepared to show this sort of initiative?

I mean really, why would we send our kid anywhere else for music lessons? This studio *rocks*.

 A **Dynamic Studio** *rocks*? 'nuff said.

What's next:

Students who feel special are students who are more likely to stay, but they still might not if the lessons themselves are a chore.

Making lessons fun is actually a very serious business: the next chapter looks at the unexpected catalysts that make fun all but inevitable, even for the most conservative of studios.

The Academy of Fun

Dial it up. Watch them stay.

The Academy of Fun

WHEN MY MIDDLE DAUGHTER WAS ABOUT 4, she saw her first ballerina on TV, was transfixed, and then spent most of the next month swan-laking about the house and breaking lamps. So we got her the tutu, the tights and the shoes, put fresh batteries in the camera, and signed her up for lessons.

It took just a few weeks for it to become clear that those classes were not going to work out; we stuck it out until the summer break hit, but then just quietly didn't re-enrol her. She never asked about it; in all honesty, she was much more excited about the tutu than she ever was about actually learning to dance (that had always been our idea, not hers).

> "...as a Dynamic Studio that's serious about *keeping students*, how serious are you about *fun?*"

Now what's interesting about this classic example of Static Studio non-retention is that the school itself was reputable, and there was nothing overtly wrong with the lessons: the teachers were thoroughly professional, the instruction of a technically high quality, the studio dance concerts impressive. But—like many schools of ballet, and more than a few music studios—it took itself far too seriously. Unforgiving of errors, fanatical about rehearsal schedules, and with classes that only ever drilled *relentlessly*, dance was the studio's number one priority, but their theory-of-mind was not sufficiently developed to understand that it's *not* the number one priority of most of the people they teach, or their time-pressed families, *and that nor should it be*.

I'm highlighting this because the same theory-of-mind problem exists for many music teachers. Of *course* music lessons are the most important thing to us: it's not just our livelihood, but a large slice of our lives, and we're continuously judged on the quality of our output. But for today's students in particular, those same lessons are a small part of a busy week, and—don't ever forget—could readily be exchanged for any one of a number of other pursuits.

So as a conscientious teacher, you'll be serious about practice, and phrasing, and dynamics, and posture, and tempo control, and repertoire choice, and precision...

...but as a Dynamic Studio that's also serious about *keeping students*, there's a further question you need to ask yourself, and one that I can't imagine my daughter's ballet school ever gave much thought to:

...how serious is your studio about *fun?*

Focusing on *catalysts*, rather than *recipes* for fun

No matter how many times the word may appear in their advertising, Static Studios have trouble creating *fun*, mostly because there are limits to just how much spontaneity is possible when lessons are driven by a policy-informed and deadline-aware todo list. With so much to get through in every session, fun can feel like the time equivalent of empty calories—and so, like a triple frosted devil's mud cake, is reserved for special occasions.

Which means that—and it will be noted by both students and parents—fun becomes the *exception.*

Dynamic Studios too can struggle; even with the additional freedom that a Dynamic approach brings, transmuting lesson time into fun is heavily dependent on elements that are not only constantly changing, but outside the teacher's control. So you might stumble on something that works for *this* student while they're *this* age, as long as you have *these* resources to hand and *this* amount of time to spare, working with *this metaphor* that's perfect for *this concept* and that happens to resonate *right now* because the student saw *this movie* recently...but those stars are very unlikely to align in exactly this way again. There can be no prescriptions for fun, because the requisite variables are myriad, context-dependent and fleeting.

It is possible, however—and this should be the goal of every Dynamic Studio—to create *conditions* where fun is likely to spontaneously germinate.

The ideas that follow are therefore not intended to be recipes so much as *catalysts,* additions to lessons that are likely to trigger your students' curiosity, and your own inner child.

That's actually then all you need: once you've got your student wondering What's Going On Today, and your own inner child running the show, fun usually takes care of itself.

So what exactly are these curiosity-making inner-child-summoning *catalysts for fun?* This chapter looks at 8 of the most potent that every music teacher should know.

Catalyst #1: Unexpected Irrelevant Curiosities (UICs)

Because we have limited physical space in our teaching studios, efficiency dictates that we should ensure everything in the room has a purpose, and can help us teach in some way. In most teaching studios, this is exactly what happens: over here are the teaching *books,* over there are the *instruments-for-hire,* over there is the *music stand,* next to that is where the *parents sit,* and the computer where the students do *theory drills,* see on the walls the *information about the next recital.* Everything in its place, and nothing superfluous to the needs of a modern and energetic teaching studio.

But if you've ever seen a young student with their nose pressed up against an aquarium, trying to get a better look at the...just what is that weird creature in there...an axolot-*what?*... or playing with a newton's cradle, or puzzling over their very first Rubik's cube, then you'll understand that there's more to making your studio fascinating than choosing the right metronome.

The key distinction here is that your studio shouldn't just be a great place to have lessons, *it should be a fun place to spend time.*

> "Static Studios struggle with fun, no matter how many times the word may appear in their advertising."

So, for example, while those start-of-lesson conversations *can* launch with something as clinical as "so...how was your practice this week", you'll have a much warmer student if it opens instead with a little to-and-fro about your new Goofy Looking Walking Fish. Within a couple of sentences they'll be telling you all about *their* pet, or a science project they once did at school, or how their big sister is afraid of snakes...all the while their parents are noting just how comfortable their child obviously is with you.

The walking fish wasn't actually the fun thing here. It was just the catalyst; the fun was in the subsequent interaction between you and the student. The catalyst is just there to trigger the interaction in the first place.

The disarming power of the UIC

This book keeps coming back to a central idea: *the Dynamic Studio is about relationships.* Teachers with solid student retention understand that there's a lot more to relating than asking how much practice their student did, and then setting about correcting intonation. But not all teachers are comfortable with producing genuinely engaging small talk—it's definitely not a strength of mine—in which case a UIC is a great starting point for such conversations. It just needs to be something that is unusual enough that it will make students curious, and the words will flow: A poster they've never seen before, with surreal art. A marble run. A lava lamp. A half completed but very large jigsaw puzzle. A compilation of ancient riddles. A *Where's Wally* print. A tapestry of knock-knock jokes. Photos of celebrities as babies, but without the names attached. Your butterfly collection. A gallery of optical illusions. Pi to 10 thousand decimal places. Magnets and a class case of iron filings. A time capsule you're about to bury. A list of names that your sister is considering for her soon-to-be-born twins. A truly unusual screensaver. Bonsai. Juggling balls.

> "...your studio shouldn't just be a great place to have lessons, *it should be a fun place to spend time.*"

What conversations will your UIC produce that might never have taken place otherwise? Which shy students will open up? How many more smiles will there be in the transitions to and from the lesson itself?

And *how much better will you get to know your students?*

For all these reasons, if I had to choose between having a metronome in my studio and having a UIC, I'd choose a UIC every time. *Every* time. (In fact, my primary interest in metronomes was in so far as they could act as a UIC, which is why I always chose unusual ones)

Ultimately though, all these curiosities and talking points are not really *Unexpected Irrelevant Curiosities.* They're *Student Retention Devices.*

Swap them over regularly, and you'll have an endless source of ice-breakers and segues...to say nothing of keeping students engaged when they're waiting, and have parents realising that there's a good deal more to you than just eighth notes and accidentals.

 The **Static Studio** knows that a *well-equipped* studio is the *mark of a professional*. The **Dynamic Studio** knows that an *interestingly-equipped* studio is a place where *students want to spend time*.

Catalyst #2: Gratuitously Engaging Repertoire (GER)

It can be hard to remember when time is at such a premium in both lessons and the practice room, but not everything you assign has to be nutritious. Some pieces won't tick any pedagogical boxes, save for the fact that they're a hoot to play...but that's actually a huge recommendation in its own right.

So that piano piece that has the performer standing up halfway through, and then ends with them *sitting* on a cluster of notes in the bottom octave might seem to have no redeeming qualities as a teaching piece (your student probably doesn't need to develop their *gluteus maximus* bass note clusters like that), but if it has the student laughing during lessons and then bouncing on and off the stage at your next recital, it's absolutely worth it.

Similarly pieces that gratuitously highlight an **unusual technique**—glissandi, or fluttertongue, or sprechstimme, or beatboxing, or prepared piano, or microtones, or snap pizzicato—can be a lot of fun for both performer and audience, while also giving you something engaging to talk about in the introduction.

Other candidates in this category are **genre bending reworkings** of well known pieces—think what Jacques Loussier was able to with JS Bach for example; Tori Amos's compellingly introspective rendition of *Smells Like Teen Spirit*; Marc-André Hamelin's *Valse Irritation d'après Nokia* (Ringtone Waltz); Flight of the Bumblebee performed by David Childs on euphonium(!)—anything that has the audience saying "wait...I *know* this one, but I've never heard it like *this*".

> "...it can be hard to remember when time is at a premium, but not everything you assign has to be nutritious."

So you *could* assign yet another first movement from a Clementi Sonatina. Or you could have the student unleash an arrangement of *The Simpson's* opening theme. Which are they more likely to practice hard? To want to be able to play in front of friends? To take a bow after on concert day?

I'm not proposing that the entire canon of repertoire for your instrument be replaced with theme music from beer commercials, but the enthusiasm generated by a fun piece can infect all the students' work—the easiest time to sell a dry diet of scales is when it's the daily payment needed to earn the right to work on The Mad Ninja Monkey's Rondo Galop.

The **Static Studio** assigns vegetables and fibre and other wholesome, nutritious repertoire. The **Dynamic Studio** occasionally also assigns deep-fried chocolate sandwiches, stardust-frosted unicorn burgers and other high-impact, low practice-resistance astonishments.

Catalyst #3: Collaborative Studio Wonders & Diversions (CSWD)

Music can be a lonely pursuit; all the more so because separate lesson times ensure that the vast majority of your students never work together. Even with an active Studio Ensemble Program (➡74), your studio is still probably working in duos, trios or quartets, and is unlikely to ever collaborate en masse on a single work.

One way to address this is by getting the whole studio to contribute to a common project; a *Studio Wonder*, if you will. It doesn't have to have anything to do with music; in fact, it will be more fun if it has nothing at all to do with the daily business of being a music student.

You might, for example, have a huge—and I mean *enormous*—box of lego in your studio, which students use to add to a communally-built and increasingly epic model. Is it a skyscraper? A spaceship? An abstract commentary on the Futility of Social Realism and Modernist Postcultural Theory? Nobody knows...but everyone who comes to their lesson will be curious to see how it's changed since last week, and then—younger students in particular—hyperventilatingly keen to add their own pieces. *How many* pieces does a student get to add after their lesson? That depends...how much did they impress you? You watch how those younger students respond when they know that being ready for the lesson means they get to add 5 pieces instead of just 1.

Alternatively, there might be a big whiteboard that hosts a growing mural, with the design growing lesson-by-lesson as students add an abstract shape here, a gnome there, a scuba-diver there, quotes from *Macbeth* over there.

Or you could have a games console set up with a driving game—every student who impresses you with how prepared they were for the lesson gets one lap at the end of their lesson, with a studiowide leaderboard for best times. Or a track editor where they get to add just one more segment of road.

Or the ongoing *Adventures of Herman The Tone-Deaf Aardvark*, a story your studio is collectively creating, and to which each student must add one sentence at the end of their lesson. By the time a student comes in for their next lesson, 35 further sentences will have been added since last time...(what's this? Herman got married, became an astronort [sic] and is being held captive on board the Pirate King's submarine! Wow!)

> "...read the entire story for the first time at your studio recital, and note just how warm the entire room feels in response."

Again, this studio project might seem *frivolous*, or a *waste of valuable lesson time*, but there is nothing frivolous about the outcome: it gets students laughing and engaged, while also creating a sense of community. If you want proof of this, read out the completed story for the first time at your studio recital, and note just how *warm* the entire room feels in response. How much better will students play now that the edge has been taken off their nerves like that? How much more generous the applause when you're not just introducing

"Sally, who is playing the Minuet"

but

"Sally—who wrote that passage where Herman *escaped* from the Pirate King's submarine by using the Invisibility Potion, and then swimming to Madagascar"?

The Adventures of Herman aside, it doesn't actually matter what your Collaborative Studio Wonder is, and adding to it doesn't need to eat up more than a minute or two of lesson time. What *does* matter is the extent to which it leaves students and parents smiling, and looking forward to their next lesson.

The **Static Studio** is an institution of excellence based on *one-on-one lessons*. The **Dynamic Studio** is an institution of excellence based on a *community*.

Catalyst #4: Shamelessly Frivolous Competitions (SFC)

We'll look in the very next chapter at the transformative impact of well-designed studio Awards, but not every competition has to target sensible core issues like student practice or performance.

You might, for example, decide to run a series of **poster competitions**—students need to submit cartoons that convey the concept of *fortissimo*. Or a *fermata*. Or *diminuendo*. Cover the walls with the entries. Use the winning entries to teach future students.

Or you might have students in October looking ridiculous as they turn up to lessons ready to take part in your **Stupid Hat of the Month awards**. Photograph the entries, post them on your walls, or Facebook page. Use it to raise money for a charity if you wish. Or not.

A Static Studio will protest that stupid hats do nothing to help a student's phrasing. They're right, but stupid hats do a huge amount to melt ice, and bring students out of themselves...which actually just *might* help their phrasing.

Again, the *content* of the contest doesn't matter; it's the fact that it's something different, unexpected, light-hearted, and *involves everyone*. Such as a **who-has-the-cutest-pet** contest. Or **whose dad looks most like Beethoven**. Or who played their instrument this month in the **most unusual location** (photos please...under a bridge? In the attic? On a gondola? In a tent? At a family reunion?)

Think laterally, think hard. You're not just creating reasons for existing students to stay, you're creating talking points which those students will share with potentially *new* students: this studio, they'll say—*your* studio—is a blast to have lessons in, I mean just look at how much goes on.

The **Static Studio** lives, breathes, thinks, eats music. The **Dynamic Studio's** world is broader, stranger and more unpredictable than that—which means everyone has a lot more fun.

Catalyst #5: Pointlessly Pompous Perpetual Honors (P³H)

In even the most Static of studios, most students will have regularly received stickers or had "great lesson!" type notes added to their lesson diary—which is precisely what makes such feedback low impact and forgettable. The currency is devalued because students who earn these rewards know that:

1) They get awards like these almost every week—no matter what they do or don't do.

2) Every other student in the studio is being given these same accolades.

221 | The Academy of Fun

3) The fact that the student has received this award is of no consequence to anybody else in the studio.

So while stickers and notes are easy to dispense, they're also not very interesting. Which means that they're not very much fun.

A Perpetual award works entirely differently. It's not *given out en masse* and then promptly *forgotten about*; it's a *scarce resource*, and is *in circulation*. Students all know the award exists, they know there's only one, and they know that every week it will go home with someone who's earned it.

So for example, you might have a *Practice Legend* scarf that goes home with the beginner student who does the most effective practice that week. If that same student is the leading practicer again next week, they get to take it home again; if not, it goes home with somebody else. But the point is that it will always be going home with *someone*, and someone deserving. Students will quickly learn what the scarf represents, and will be genuinely excited and proud whenever it's theirs.

Perpetual Awards are high impact, but in of themselves are not what's fun—again, they're just a catalyst. This time what's key for the fun factor is not just the award itself, but the *hype that surrounds the presentation:*

Hayley, this has been outstanding week of practice. In fact...wait there...

...and moments later the Practice Scarf is being carried into the room on a cushion, with a recording of Pomp and Circumstance running in the background—the more over-the-top the moment, the bigger the grins from student and parents. The winner knows what's next: they get to put it on, pose for the Official Photo, make a thank-you speech ("...couldn't have done this without my parents; I want also to thank my little sister for..."), the transcript to go in your next Studio Newsletter. And then they get to wear it not just home, but *everywhere* that week, sending in photos of where the scarf has been, as though they were their own paparazzi.

It's insane overkill for such a small award. That's the point.

Whatever criteria you might end up using to create such perpetual awards, the very fact that they exist is a fun and unorthodox way to congratulate deserving students—and the hype that accompanies their issue is yet another off-beat way your studio keeps students engaged, motivated and guessing.

The **Static Studio** understands that a ticker-tape parade and airforce flyby is overkill just because a student wins Student Of The Week. The **Dynamic Studio** understands that too, but will do it anyway.

Catalyst #6: Pointlessly Engaging Games (PEG)

Games are compelling to work with because of the associated verb. You *play* a game. You don't have to *correct* a game or *practice* a game until it's right or any of the other verbs that otherwise constitute so much of our teaching lexicon and drudgify lessons.

They're also endlessly versatile: games can be used with almost any lesson task, but come into their own particularly when students need to *cement* a solution by *repeating* it. Reframed as a game, the process not only works more efficiently, but without the attendant pain; if a student is tasked with looping a corrected fingering twenty times they might as well be *moving around a board* while they do it, or *collecting cards*, or *stacking blocks*, or *pinning tails on a donkey*, or *moving a stick figure up a ladder*.

So there's nothing actually "pointless" about these games: while the underlying pedagogical mechanics of games might not always be transparent to the student, they nonetheless relentlessly direct the student's behavior towards achieving desired outcomes.

The fact that Static Studios choose not to work so much with games is not because they lack the requisite creativity or a sense of fun, but because setting up games can seem all a bit too untidy and time-consuming: all those *cards* and *dice* and *markers* and *tokens*.

> **"...games are systems, and are without peer as a way to convey information and build skills."**

But it only requires a shift in thinking to launch a game, not the procurement of an equipment list; essentially a game is simply a conceptual *repackaging* of problems, converting the otherwise abstract corrections you need into vividly measurable and imagination-infused challenges. With the target clear, and the student motivated to get there, the fact that it also happens to be *fun* is almost incidental: games are *systems*, and without peer as a way to convey information and build skills.

So far from requiring sophisticated resources, launching a game can be as simple as starting a sentence with "Hey, I bet you can't..." —as surely as "Did not" will be followed by "Did too", "I bet you can't" is almost always followed by "I bet I *can*", particularly if you choose your student carefully, and then set your challenge as something that's *just* out of reach, and thefore demands they be their best:

> I bet you can't play this passage with your eyes closed/at 75 beats per minutes/with the dynamics reversed/while you say

your 7 times table/a semi-tone lower than written/all in on breath/five times in a row with the new fingering in/10 times correctly in 5 minutes...

Whether you opt for these sorts of instantly declared and ephemeral I-bet-you-can't-based challenges, or a more official looking tailored-for-this-student dice-and-markers contest, the value of having rebundled your feedback into a game should be evident in the post lesson reports. When the student is asked "what did you do today?", instead of them saying:

I played that hard bit in the Sonatina a bazillion times.

Their report is:

We played Zombie Asteroid Disasters. Then we played *Ultra Zombie Asteroid Disasters*. It was *awesome*, especially the part where I got to smash down the lego tower because I got that bit in the Sonatina right enough times in a row, and I smashed it so hard that the piece flew over the other side of the room and went into the fish tank. It was sooo funny.

Note that both approaches actually had the student looping the troublesome passage over and over. So it was the same outcome either way, but a completely different experience: that's not just a *happy* student, that's an *engaged* student—and a student who will be quick to tell their parents "my music lessons are *fun*".

 The **Static Studio** believes that music lessons should be dignified, with an air of gravitas appropriate to the artistic legacy for which we are merely custodians. The **Dynamic Studio** wants another game of *Zombie Asteroid Disasters*, at least until *Mutant Viking Snowboarders* comes out.

Catalyst #7: Unwarranted Hyperbolic Metaphors (UHM)

For younger children in particular, Unwarranted Hyperbolic Metaphors are a great way not only to get them smiling, but to ensure concepts stick without having to limit yourself to the decidedly un-fun default language of music. Of course, it's a rare teacher that doesn't call upon metaphors, but the key here is dialling them up to a point of vivid absurdity.

So young students don't think it's fun to be told to play the fortissimo passage *loudly*. They do think it's somewhat fun when you challenge them to play loudly enough to *make pictures fall off the walls*. And more fun still when you don't mean the walls of *your studio*, but the walls of the building *next door*.

Similarly, they don't think it's fun to be told to play *staccatissimo*; they do think it's somewhat fun to be told to produce a sound so short, so sharp, it can *burst a balloon*. More fun still if you blow up a *real balloon* so they can actually try it for themselves.

Turning abstract details into conceivable but actually physically impossible challenges will have most students laughing at the hyperbole, but then focusing on the musical element in question with everything they've got: unlike someone who was simply told to "write out what this word means 5 times", the balloon student in the example above will never forget what *staccatissimo* requires. Again, there is astonishing potential for *information retention* in *fun*.

The **Static Studio** recognises the power of an apt metaphor as a vehicle for reinforcing musical concepts
The **Dynamic Studio** think that metaphors invented by Wil-e-Coyote will stay in young student's minds longer.

Catalyst #8: Randomisation (1D6)

Not every lesson element needs to unfold with Olympic Game Opening Ceremony planning and precision. One very easy way to make what-happens-next a good deal more fun is to occasionally make it thoroughly *unpredictable*.

What if, for example—just for a couple of weeks—practice challenges were not written in a book, but *drawn from a hat?* Or *unwrapped*, like presents, before each practice session? Or *sent as a series of texts*, like instructions from a Spy Agency Headquarters (your missions, should you choose to accept them, appearing each day at exactly 6pm)?

What if the *order of attack* of a lesson (➡ 2 5) was determined by a spin of a wheel?

> Scales | Theory | Etude | Sonata | Competition Piece | Improvisation |

Or a similar wheel to determine *which element* to target today within a particular piece:

> Intonation | Rhythmic Precision | Score Details | Tempo Control | Tone Production

Or another such wheel to determine the *extent and nature* of the immediate challenge:

> eyes closed | at half tempo | pausing at the end of every phrase | exaggerated dynamics | absent/flat dynamics | all dynamics inverted | 10% faster that you'd normally want to perform it |

The promise throughout a lesson like this? That the *next* three minutes will always be completely different from the three minutes that preceded it.

Still not fun enough for them? It's your wheel. You can add whatever fresh options you like.

| help yourself to a chocolate |

or

| take a ticket in the Studio Raffle |

or

| my teacher is not allowed to say any words with the letter "e" in them for the rest of the lesson |

Stupid? Yes. Fun? Absolutely. Compulsory? No—and this is important to understand—you're in charge of when and how often such silliness appears. If your instincts are warning you not to mix things up too much for a particular student, then so be it. Dynamic doesn't mean *arbitrary* or *flippant* or *oblivious*.

Bigger picture, the question is this: *what sort of studio do you want to be known for?* Do you rate laughter and a spring in a student's step as being at least as important as consistent tone production?

And if not—seriously, and I'm happy to debate the point in person if we ever meet—why on earth would you be teaching in the first place?

 The **Static Studio** prefers not to think too hard about that question, they're tired enough as it is. The **Dynamic Studio** knows that *tired* is caused by a deficiency of *fun*.

What's next:

In an age when computer games track, highlight, chronicle and broadcast the player's every breakthrough—big and small—the lines between *fun* and *progression* get blurred in a way that has hugely exciting implications for anyone involved in education.

Earlier in this book we looked at techniques for creating *evidence of progress;* in this chapter, we've just looked at a selection of *catalysts for creating fun...*

...just how motivated might students become if you were to fuse the two? One possible result would be a Studio Awards scheme; the next chapter is a tour of how it might work.

Dynamic Rewards

The power of Achievements-based accolades

Dynamic Rewards

IN AN AGE WHERE STUDENTS ARE used to working with sophisticated and addictive computer game achievements systems, a
meaningful and well-designed Awards system can be a peerless
student retention tool. We looked in the previous chapter at
one such possibility; a well-hyped Perpetual Award system
(➡ 220-222), as an alternative to the quickly-forgotten same-old
system of simply issuing stickers.

However, there is a danger in working only with Perpetual
Awards. By definition, they're a *scarce resource*—there can only
be one Student of the Month, or
Practice Champion—so every time
you hand out such an award, a lot of
students are left feeling overlooked.
So if these are the *only* type of
awards available, while they're busy
doing their job encouraging the
select few, they can also be actively
desensitizing, and then ultimately
discouraging the bulk of your studio.
Students learn that rewards are not
for *me*, they're for *other people.*

> "There are few studio retention ideas for today's students more potent—or motivating—than making this shift."

Unfortunately, as any economist will tell you, resolving this
is not as simple as manufacturing extra awards, because it's the
very scarcity which confers value. Sending everyone home with
a prize will ensure that...well, it will ensure that *everyone gets a
prize*, but the prizes themselves won't be sought after, valued,
recommended or remembered. Your "awards" will be ephemeral
in their impact, kindling tossed onto embers, generating little
heat.

This seems to leave teachers with an invidious choice: ensure your Awards system retains the *value* of rewards, but disenfranchise most of your studio in the process, or give your Awards *junk bond status* by making sure that everyone gets one.

As computer game designers know only too well, it's a false dilemma though. Valuable rewards don't have to be for the select few, nor do universally available awards have to be without value. The Dynamic Studio solution is to stop reserving awards as being the exclusive preserve of *podium-finishers*, and instead start treating them as something that can be *earned*.

There are few studio retention ideas for today's students more potent—or motivating—than making this shift. Let's take a look at how it works.

The power of earnable awards

The idea behind earnable awards is that eligibility is clearly defined, and then *any student who ticks all the necessary boxes will become an automatic recipient.* Here it's not scarcity that confers value, but the fact that the awards must be *earned*, much like a badge in scouts, or a university degree. You can dial up or down the perceived value not by limiting supply, but by controlling how demanding those qualifications are.

So, for example, you might have an award that focuses on *public performance*—as soon as a student has participated in 10 recitals, they might receive a Recital Veteran award. Or there might be an award similarly focused on *practice*, available to anyone who turns up to 12 lessons in a row with everything asked for prepared. Or another for *technical work* that students can earn by being able to play a set list of scales at a set tempo.

The most immediate benefit is inclusivity: rather than simply benefiting those who were first across the finish line, *these awards are available to anyone who completes all the checkpoints in the race.* In that way, your students aren't divided into winners and losers; they're split into "have earned the reward" and "haven't earned the reward *yet.*"

It sounds like a semantic shift, but it's fundamentally different psychologically for students who take part, and unlocks some exciting Dynamic Studio possibilities.

Highlighting your studio's values

Because your earnable rewards are criteria based, the content of that criteria is completely up to you. Your choices—what you *focus on*, the *breadth and depth of the requirements*, what you *omit entirely*—will say more about your teaching than any advertisement ever could. List an Award, and it's impossible for parents not to start making assumptions about your studio:

- If your studio offers awards for **completing sightreading challenges**, then parents will assume that your studio is interested in helping its students become strong sight-readers, and—by extension—that students who stay in your studio will *become* strong sight readers.

- Add a lengthy chain of **practice milestone** awards, and parents will know that you take practice seriously.

- Create awards for **completing technical work** challenges (*Scales Bootcamp* at insidemusicteaching.com is an example of this taken to extremes), and parents will know that you value technical development, and are prepared to be creative in pursuit of that end.

• Offer a **wide variety** of awards that cater to a range of skills, and parents will know that your studio values accommodating and developing individual strengths; offer just a **few,** but in *great depth,* and parents will assume your studio is *the* place to go to master those particular elements.

So defining Awards is as much a strategic decision dictating how you want your studio to be perceived as it is laying the foundations for studio retention; the two are, of course, closely linked.

The **Static Studio** uses *adjectives in advertisements* to *talk up its strengths.*
The **Dynamic Studio** makes its values *self evident* by the *Awards it creates.*

Solving problems

If students in your studio tend to struggle with the same type of problem—say, for example difficulty in *reading rhythm,* in a studio that otherwise loves to work with *contemporary popular repertoire*—then criteria-based awards are an ideal way both to turn the problem around, and stem the associated loss of students.

So in this case, you might have a series of graded Rhythm Reading challenges, which students would now not be doing just because it's *good for you* (the shut-up-and-just-eat-your-broccoli technique) but because there's an *Award waiting for you once you're done* (the ice-cream-for-finishing-what's-on-your-plate strategy). With solid incentives in place for students to focus on rhythm reading, it's almost inconceivable that rhythm reading wouldn't improve across the studio...which in turn means fewer students not being able to get their head around it...which means fewer students not coping with the repertoire that depended on those skills...which means fewer discouraged students...

...which means fewer *ex*-students.

The targetted issues don't have to be musical; they can be anything at all that annoys or frustrates or even so much as *inconveniences* you about your job. This whole book has been about refusing to accept such negatives as being inevitable or permanent: Awards are a potent soft-force way of nudging your students and their families to the changes you need.

> "...when those questions turn into a brand new Award, your students will be blissfully unaware of the thinking behind it"

So if you have students who are driving you insane by constantly *arriving late*, but who you don't want to discourage by lecturing or punishing, then create *incentives* for *arriving on time*.

So in this instance, your Award criteria might be:

any student who turns up to an entire Semester of lessons without being late once;

the reward might be :

goes in the draw to receive a 25% fee discount next semester

Any parent who sees *that* is going to work very hard to ensure their child is on time, and you've achieved it without a single angry word.

All studios have frustrations; instead of just complaining about them, a Dynamic Studio is likely to list them, and then ask themselves two questions:

"What does this problem **look like** once it's **solved?**" and

"How can I create a series of **Award criteria** that **incentivise that outcome?**"

When those questions turn into a brand new Award, your students will be blissfully unaware of the thinking behind it, and will just be focused on the prize itself. In reality though, this whole exercise has been a strategic deployment.

The **Static Studio** handles problems by *enforcing mandated changes.*
The **Dynamic Studio** handles problems by *creating incentives for change.*

Creating a future for students to work towards

As we looked at in the Diversified Studio chapter, many online computer games only make money when players stay subscribed over a period of time, and so they've become very good at ensuring that players have huge chains of *time consuming* but *motivating* tasks to get through. (➡ 58-59)

Any game designer will confirm that if you set up a compelling system of Studio Awards, students are going to be pulled forwards; because most of the Awards are *in the future*, the student will have to *stick around until then* to earn them:

> I only have 7 more challenges to complete to earn this huge Award, I've already completed 23, I might as well see it through.

> I've just earned my Silver Award. I know that the Gold Award students end up with their name on the honor board. I want my name there, I might as well see it through.

Or the following piece of shameless bribery:

> Every time I earn a new studio Award, I get a ticket in the Studio Lucky Dip End Of Year Raffle. I know that in that prize pool somewhere is a new games console(!), and a family pass to "Vertigo! Rollercoaster World". I want to earn *lots* of tickets so I have the best chance possible when the draw is done at the end-of-year recital.

To create the prize pool for that last idea might cost you the equivalent of one-and-a-half student's worth of fees for a whole year, something no Static Studio would consider. But if the whole thing fires up your studio so much that it causes *6 students* to stay who otherwise might have left, then it has paid for itself many, many times over.

Three very different motivations, but in each case, the student has the promise of a reward simply by continuing to stay the path.

If you think about it though, the mantra of "work for an extended period of time to earn a reward" is really not so different from "practice over a number of years to become proficient on your instrument". It's just more immediate, easier to understand.

But the growing trophy cabinet is more than just a compendium of congratulations; because your Awards are criteria based, they're also powerful evidence of progress. Every new Award represents a new skillset tamed; with a steady stream of new skill-based Awards coming in, their child is obviously learning plenty with you—why would anyone *stop* that?

The **Static Studio** believes that all student motivation should be *intrinsic*.
The **Dynamic Studio** nudges students with *external* and decidedly *non-musical incentives*.

An example of how to set up Criteria-Based Awards

For criteria-based awards to work, a number of elements have to be in place: the awards need titles that in of themselves *generate excitement* and *suggest progression*; the criteria need to leave students clear on *exactly what's required*; the very first award needs a *low and readily achievable qualification mark*, so participants can taste early success; and thereafter, there needs to be a series of *upgrades* available that become *exponentially more difficult*.

> "...because your Awards are criteria based, they're also powerful evidence of progress."

That might all sound a bit abstract. To anyone who plays computer games though, it will feel very familiar—it's a tested, and highly addictive formula. Let's see how it might work in the context of music lessons:

Setting the scene—and expectations—with the award's *title*

Let's imagine that the skill you want to promote is **key signature recognition**. You *could* create an award simply called:

> Key Signature Proficiency Award

That's *accurate*. But it's also *bland*, and contains nothing that suggests any sort of *progression*.

For our purposes, much more likely to fire the imagination, and also hint at further rewards to come, would be something like:

> Key Signature Ninja (1st Degree)

There's more to this than just a cutesy title. Not only is the over-the-top-hype disarming for older students and engaging for younger students, it inevitably has everybody wondering: what comes *after* 1st degree?

What indeed. The beauty of introducing numbers into series like this is that they can run as deep as you need, and can also easily be extended. So if your original Award set caps out at 5th Degree, but you have a dozen students who have finished that and are clamouring for more, then you can create a 6th. And a 7th. And so on—it's a system that is *dynamic*.

Defining the qualifications

…remember, it's your award, so you get to decide the criteria. But as any computer game developer will tell you, it's important not to make the first award too hard to get. Challenging, but accessible, with not too much time between *started playing* and *earned your very first reward*. So one possibility for this initial Key Signature award might be:

• To have scored 90% or more on the Official Studio Key signature Challenge Sheet Level 1 (Tests up to 3 sharps and flats)

• Correctly identify the key signatures of 15 randomly chosen works. (again, up to three sharps and flats)

That's it. The requirements are light because you want students to experience that the system *works*: complete the tasks, get your reward.

Notice also that the criteria is clearly stated in advance, so that when students are considering working towards becoming a 1st Degree Key Signature Ninja they know exactly what is involved. Students are allowed as many attempts as they need. So they can't be discouraged by having the award permanently unavailable to them; but nor are you coddling them by giving rewards they haven't yet earned. Once they've met all the criteria—however long it took them—the reward is theirs.

Make a fuss, congratulate them, post the achievement somewhere prominent for all to see.

And then immediately—and this is the core of using Awards as retention devices—*issue them with a chance to upgrade*. You've given them a taste of the tick-these-things-to-earn-your-Award; now you get them hooked.

Laying out upgrade paths

So what do your students do once they have earned their Key Signatures Ninja (1st Degree) award? That will pretty much take care of itself. They'll be eyeing the Key Signatures Ninja (2nd Degree)

(You did design one, right?) Much more prestigious, as not so many students have their name on that honour board. And of course, there's a 3rd Degree available too, but it's *really* tough to get.

So this new 2nd Degree Award would be similar to the 1st Degree award, except that this time they might have to

score 100% on a sheet that tests *all* key signatures,

correctly identify the key signatures of *100* randomly chosen works(!) in *any* key, and

pass a timed key signature quiz (there are online versions of these quizzes for free at InsideMusicTeaching.com)

Obviously it's going to take much, much longer to work through the 2nd Degree requirements: as it should. But any students who have completed them all not only deserve the award, but will be well on top of their key signatures. And that, right there, is what's so important about the transition to a Dynamic Studio: you're not *dumbing anything down*, or *expecting less*, or *seeking merely to entertain*. Your standards can (and should) be stratospheric; it's just that you're making it much more likely that students will actually get there. They just don't have to go straight into orbit as their very first challenge.

I haven't listed sample 3rd degree requirements. You get the idea. If you use your imagination, you can create plenty of upgrade paths, ensuring that the early ones are readily attainable, while the highest honours require efforts of Herculean proportions.

How many categories and upgrades should you create? The more the better; it helps the students to feel as though they have genuine options, ensuring that their collection of awards is different from those of other students. So under the system above, one student might have earned their 4th degree Musical Terms and Signs, but only their 1st Degree on Rhythm Reading. Her friend might have completed the requirements for 2nd Degree on Rhythmic Dictation, but ticked all the boxes necessary for 6th Degree (godlike! The only student in the studio!) on Sightreading.

(You can see how broad and deep an Awards structure can run in my book *Scales Bootcamp*, which features over three thousand(!) Achievements for pianists to earn as they master their scales...again, from entry level simple through to brain-and-finger-crunchingly evil.)

Other possibilities for Awards

The beauty of criteria-based rewards is that the criteria are defined by you, according to emerging needs—rather than, say, an exam syllabus, which is constructed by a distant committee who knows nothing about your studio, or the students you teach.

So having looked at the structure that can underpin awards, what could your awards be for?

Let's look at just a few: the options really are limitless.

Encouraging performance experience

This is designed to encourage students to air their pieces publicly *before* they really need them, and also give them credit for actually playing their pieces in front of people.

The idea is that they score one point for every person who hears them play their piece, so the bigger the audience, the more points they can rack up. A performance for their family might earn them 5 points. If they play it for their class at school, they might earn 28 points. An assembly performance can be worth hundreds.

Your studio might then offer Public Performance Awards for 50 points, 200 points and 500 points. And yes, repeat concerts still count, while the points are cumulative. So if they organise to give a "performance" just to their parents every night for a week, they will end up with 14 Performance Points for that.

It is not unreasonable to expect that a student with 1200 performance points behind them is going to be much calmer about playing that piece on competition day that one who only has 10 performance points.

In fact, you may want to mandate a minimum amount of points that they should earn before they even *think* about playing these pieces in that big competition or exam...or your showcase end-of-year recital, for that matter...

Getting them focused on the future: repertoire milestones

In the same way that football players are given a special reception by the crowd on the occasion of their 50th international game, there should be some recognition of the 50th piece that a student has learned with you. And an even bigger accolade for their 100th. Apart from helping them to be proud of what they have already done, it has them focussing on the idea that one day they would like to be a member of the prestigious "200 Club". Of course, to do that, they are going to have to stick around until then.

Creating behavior out of nothing: Getting students to live concerts

Your studio awards might look like an elaborate structure for boosting student's self-esteems, but they're actually about shaping student *behaviour*. Whatever your Awards criteria are becomes what your students will *do*.

This means that if you find yourself frustrated by something your students *aren't* doing, then instead of merely complaining to them, or making recommendations, ask yourself how you might turn the desired change into an awards structure.

So for example, you might have noticed that—despite a wealth of opportunities—that very few of your students attend live concerts.

Having stated the problem, possibilities for criteria for the Award all but suggests itself: your students would earn points for every concert they attend. *Double* points if they go with other students. *Triple* points if they write a summary of what they experienced while they were there—the elements in the playing they liked, the things they didn't, and why. Again, once they have accumulated a pre-defined number of points they qualify for the award.

What's important here is then not the reward itself, but the benefits that the resultant change in behavior brings. If this turns some students into temporary concert junkies just to pursue an Award, then so be it—what they gain enormously outweighs any debates over lack of honour in their motivation. But in the mix will be some students who have just established a habit—and a true reward—that will last a lifetime.

243 | Dynamic Rewards

Targeting the days *between* lessons: Practice Awards

Practicing lends itself to a dizzying range of possible awards—too many to fit in this chapter, so I've posted a free online guide to running a Practice Competition at InsideMusicTeaching. com.

Manipulating student perception of timelines

Nothing prompts discussions of maybe-it's-time-to-stop-lessons quite like an embarrassingly bad recital performance. Unfortunately, we've all got students who like to delay their preparation until they can see the whites of the deadline's eyes—this then prompts a week of panic cramming practice (which stresses everyone involved) followed by a disaster anyway (ditto).

An Award that encourages students to not only be ready for their deadlines, but to be ready *early* can help minimise the number of students who sabotage their performances like this.

The idea is that not just a few days but *two weeks* before the actual date, they would have a mock recital. If they pull it off, then they automatically qualify for the Award.

That's for the silver version. For the gold version, they might need to be ready a *month* ahead of schedule.

They still might be panic practicing to suit up for these Awards, but at least that panic practice is happening long before the actual deadline—the whole exercise is paralleled in the building industry, where progress on a major contract might be assessed a year ahead of the final deadline, with incentives for being ahead of schedule, and penalties for being behind. Whatever the outcome, if things *are* behind where they should be, there's still time to do something about it.

Redefining their assumptions about limits

Earlier in the book, we looked at disrupting the student's workload expectations by occasionally giving them a monster intray, and then a horribly tight deadline to get through it all—say, for example, a public performance in only a fortnight of a tough piece they've only just been given today.

Given the scale of these demands, you might create a special Award which awaits students who take on—and then survive—such challenges.

Make a fuss over *this* year's recipients of the Nightmare Fortnight Challenge Award, and you'll end up with even more students who take it on *next* year.

Over to you...

You could ignore all of the suggested Awards in this book, and still come up with dozens of brilliant options of your own. The key point though is that necessity is the mother of invention in each case: your Awards are not simply Arbitrary Good Ideas You've Had, but calculated responses to changes, problems and opportunities in your studio.

In fact, any archeologist studying your studio should be able to deduce the various challenges that faced your studio, just by looking at the Awards students were able to earn.

The **Static Studio** uses Awards to *reward* students for good work.
The **Dynamic Studio** uses Awards to *solve problems*, and *puppetmaster* student behavior.

Choosing compelling Award vehicles

Ok, so you've established the criteria for all your studio Awards, and your students have just been unleashed in pursuit.

Sooner or later, they're going to catch one. And when they do, you had better be ready—it's not going to be enough to simply pat them on the head and say "congratulations", otherwise they may not feel inclined to chase next year's Awards so hard.

This means that you need to be budgeting for suitably engaging awards. The money spent is not money *forgone*, but *invested* with the expectation of a return: remember, if it costs you an entire year of fees from one student to fund your Awards, but those awards help you retain *two* students, then you're in front.

So what form can rewards take? Let's look at some of the options—familiar and unfamiliar—and how to get the most out of each medium.

Honour Boards

You *could* highlight awardee's names with just a sheet of cardboard and a marker, but if you want your honour boards to seem official, then they have to look that way. Find a wall in the studio, make your measurements, then contact a local business that specialises in producing timber honor boards.

You'll be able to have the name and/or logo of your studio, together with a series of columns, one for each Award type. To add names, just contact the company each time with the details, and they'll send you a lettered version of what you need—you just stick the names directly onto the board as needed.

Initial cost is steep—this is an investment that can cost hundreds of dollars—but thereafter the cost is minimal as you order each new name. Given the costs though, you normally would save these boards for only your highest level Awards; unless you have very deep pockets and very long walls, this is not the way to highlight your Students Of The Week.

There are two reasons it's worth going to the trouble and the expense of honor boards though. First of all, they add legitimacy to your Awards—there's something permanent and trustworthy about the honor board, like ivy growing on a school.

And secondly, being listed on there will feel like a Big Deal. Those students whose name is not yet there will be trying to work out how it can be. Parents who see their kids' name listed there will be as proud as—well, parents of a kid whose name has been listed on an honor board. It's a win all round.

Certificates

Like the honour boards, if you want your certificates to seem official, then you need to design them (or have them designed) specifically for *your* studio and *this* purpose, otherwise they'll look mass produced, generic and forgettable. Make sure your studio logo or name is prominent enough to be read from a few feet away—remember, these Awards are likely to go on the student's fridge, or be taken in to school for show and tell, and you should not miss the opportunity for a little promotion.

Design these well once, and all you'd need to change in the future is the name of the recipient and the title of the Award— the rest can stay as is each time, both ensuring consistency, and saving you design time.

If you get stuck, there are predesigned certificate templates freely available at InsideMusicTeaching.com, but if you have the design skills (and every music teacher should), by far the best option is to work with a specialised design program like Adobe's Indesign, and produce it yourself. Alternatively, you can commission professionally designed certificates through a website like 99designs.com for a fraction of the cost of hiring a graphic designer.

Stickers

Stickers are forgettable when they're simply a "well done" message stuck on a book, but compelling when they're something that can be *collected*. The key to getting students excited about stickers is to cultivate a sense of *incompleteness*, focusing not on the stickers they already have, but those they could be earning in the future.

As each new sticker is earned, trace an outline in their book of where the sticker they could be getting next would go... and then be specific about what they need to do to earn it. The ghosted sticker will play on their minds, and they will be very keen to replace it with the real thing.

You can take this even further by tracing in the outline of entire **sets of stickers**. For students of particular personality types (you know the students I mean), this prospect of collect-them-all can prove an irresistible goal...particularly if collecting them all then qualifies the student for another Award in its own right. Or a listing on an honor board. Or another ticket in your end-of-year-studio-raffle. Or whatever.

Book of Achievements

Again, this feeds on the very human desire to collect, and is a tactic used by just about every computer game on the planet. The idea here is to create a book that lists *every* Award your studio offers and the associated criteria, together with a space for you to sign and date the occasion that the student qualifies for each. The book itself will end up both as an ongoing record of *what they've achieved so far*, and a potent temptation for *what's ahead*.

Books like this are issued to students, but for retention purposes, the students are not actually the target. When their *parents* read through a book like that—packed as it is with Awards their child can earn—they're being made very aware of the cost of stopping lessons; the book is not just a Awards Prospectus, but *a compendium of what's yet to do*, and what their child would miss out on, were they so shortsighted as to leave your studio.

Badges

It's a tactic stolen straight from Boy Scouts: instead of a certificate book, your students would have an Awards T-shirt. The shirt will be plain when they start—perhaps with the logo of your studio—but any rewards you issue will be small cloth badges, which will be sewn or ironed onto their Awards T-Shirt.

Younger students may even wear the T-shirt to lessons, as they turn themselves into a walking Awards billboard. At a glance, you can then see the triangular badges that signify Rhythm Reading quests have been complete, the octagons of Consistent Practice, and the blue rectangles of One Dozen Performances Given.

Older students will probably feel encumbered by too much dignity to wear anything like that, but will still hang on to the garment for years to come—it's exactly the sort of thing they will discover again when they are moving house in twenty years time, and should produce a rush of fond memories.

And when I consider the things I had to do to get my Bushcraft Level 1 Badge when I was a cub scout, practicing a musical instrument would have felt like a much better option. (Can you light a fire with nothing more than a damp stick, a rock, 25 ml of wombat urine and a handful of eucalyptus leaves? No? Neither could I. Give me a G major scale any day)

There's more to print on than just paper

There will be a store at your local mall that allows you to print pictures onto t-shirts or mugs...or baseball hats, calendars, jigsaw puzzles, key rings, mousepads...

Don't forget to enquire about bulk rates: one especially engraved Pencil of Notereading Excellence might be prohibitively expensive, but if you were to order 100 of them, not only would you have saved money, but you now have a three year supply. That might seem excessive, but if you have plans for lots of your students to qualify for Notereading Excellence awards (and why wouldn't you?) then you need plenty of such awards to hand.

Presentation Options

If you want your students to take the awards seriously, you need to be seen to be taking them seriously. If Oscars were simply Fed-ex'ed to the recipients, together with a letter of congratulations, nobody would pay attention to Academy Awards.

There are several ways that you can help these Awards feel larger than life:

Put it in the Newsletter

Don't just use your studio newsletter to tell students about term dates and concert venues. Have a section permanently reserved for spelling out the Award Winners this month. This means that not only did you personally tell them how proud you were, but you are now telling the rest of the studio too.

Add to your Honor Boards

Most people aren't going to end up with suburbs named after them, or have their own likeness at Madame Tussaudes, which is exactly why we all get such a thrill from seeing our own names engraved. Exciting for those already named, and a tantalising possibility for those who aren't on there yet.

Post it on your webpage

If your studio has its own webpage, make sure details of Awards are front and center. Again, it's about making the accolade public, and now, the whole planet can see it.

...but really, you should hold an Awards Night

At the end of every year, consider introducing a little red carpet magic to your studio. Book out a restaurant or a hall (don't feel bad about levying a fee per head for attending), organise for some students to perform during the evening, or better yet, to wait on tables. (truly!) Chat to parents, laugh with your students, and enjoy the food.

And then, in the moment where speeches would normally appear at a wedding reception, lower the houselights, put on Elgar's *Pomp and Circumstance*, open the envelopes and call the winners to the podium. Be generous in your summary of each student's achievements, and then remind everyone about how this fits in with the bigger picture: Here's what we did this year. This is why it was important. Here's how brilliantly your kids coped with it all.

Here's a short performance from one of our best students. And another from one of our newest. And another from one of our most rapidly improving.

And if you thought the past 12 months were exciting, you won't believe what we have planned for next year. Here's a sneak preview. Here are some dates for your calendar.

Have a safe break. I'm itching to find out just what's possible for your child when we get back...

...what's a wavering parents to do after a night like that? Are they really prepared to put an end to all this?

What's next:

While it's possible to create compelling Studio Awards with minimal resources, well-equipped studios definitely have an advantage when it comes to manufacturing fun or feedback of any type.

The go-to word always seems to be "technology"; what's exciting though is not the gadgets, but the possibilities they unlock. Don't be fooled by sticker price: $300 worth of entry level equipment in the hands of a teacher focused on how to turn that *technology* into *compelling lessons* is much, much more valuable than $25,000 worth of state-of-the-art in the hands of a teacher who *has* it, but never really figures out what it's *for*.

The next chapter looks at technology options that every studio should consider, and—of more interest to the Dynamic Studio—takes you on a tour of what you might actually *do* with it all.

Dynamic Resourcing
The well equipped studio

Dynamic Resourcing

THIS BOOK STARTED WITH A THOUGHT experiment based around tearing down your studio, and then rebuilding it from scratch. Let's refine that for a moment, zoom in just on the *resources* you'd need, and reframe the question a little:

If you were moving to a new city, having left all your possessions behind, what would you need to get for your studio so you could do your job?

For most teachers, the answer is uncomplicated, functional, and is all about addressing the immediate needs of traditional lessons:

A music stand. A chair for the teacher, another for anyone watching. Metronome somewhere. Music books. Manuscript paper. Pencils.

An instrument to demonstrate on.

Student standing where X marks the spot. Teacher sitting in the teaching chair. Ready to go.

You could certainly run lessons with resources like that. So could the person who taught you, or the person who taught *them*. Which is exactly what's wrong with this picture.

Advances in technology are constantly opening new teaching possibilities that were unthinkable when you were having your first lessons. Constantly opening, that is, assuming you have the gear you need, and—critically—have some idea what it's *for*.

This is different from simply knowing how to *operate* the equipment. When Sony or Apple or Steinberg or whoever put together their instruction manuals, they include plenty of information on how to *use* the device in the box, but not how to *teach* with it. Unless you're clear on the latter, it's just a gadget...but once you *are* clear...oh my. Your job, your entire studio, *transforms*.

Being able to afford what you need: the "technology tax"

The biggest obstacle to a Dynamic Studio equipping itself with the technology it needs is still the cost of the resources—music teachers are not often seen playing polo with their art dealer. But it's a mistake to think of the price of technology for your studio as a *cost*; it's actually an *investment*. Having these resources not only increases your ability to keep the students you already have, it gives you new selling points to help attract students to the studio in the first place.

One way forwards is to set aside a percentage of student takings to make it possible. This growing technology fund—a self imposed technology tax, if you will—will, over time, make some astonishing resources and new teaching options possible.

> "...you *could* run lessons with resources like that. So could the person who taught you...or the person who taught *them*."

As you then start to triage your way through the purchase decisions, don't get seduced by the gadgets themselves. Look instead at the teaching solutions they make possible, and then rank those—in the end, it's *solutions* you're purchasing, not *gadgetry*.

That said, there is one item that you do need to take care of first, because almost everything else depends on it.

It all starts with a good computer

A lot of music studios save money by getting the cheapest non-stolen computer they can, and then hanging on to it until birds start nesting in the case. The problem with this is that the 7-year old clunker that you then word-process on is not going to cut it for the sort of audio, video and image processing that we'll be talking about in the rest of this chapter.

In short, unless you bought a good computer in the past few years, it's almost pointless making any other technological upgrade.

I'm not talking about throwing in extra RAM or a bigger hard drive into an old computer; that's just lipstick on a pig. I'm talking about a new system with enough horsepower to get you through the next half-decade of work.

I don't want to get into Mac vs PC (I'm an enthusiastic macuser after two decades of struggling with PCs, and wouldn't be at all impartial), but whatever you choose, choose *something*, and choose it as soon as you're able. There are excellent Mac and PC versions of all the types of software that I'm about to talk about, so you win either way, and a whole new world opens once you've got a good computer at your studio's core.

If you're bewildered by specs, get advice, but *not* from whoever is selling the computer—get it from people who actually *use* the sort of software you'll be working with. So if you're planning on doing your own studio recordings, talk to a store that sells music software, or better yet, talk to an actual recording studio or commercial composer that depends on good hardware for a living.

The **Static Studio** laments that they can't afford to keep up with technology. The **Dynamic Studio** knows that they can't afford *not* to.

How to learn how to use all this stuff

That's obviously well beyond the scope of this book, but you can teach yourself just about anything you need to know, as long as you have an internet connection and are prepared to put in the time.

Most of what you'll need to master is not actually *gadgets* but *software*, which is actually much easier to get your head around—just go to on online training website like Lynda.com or VTC.com, and you'll see thousands of training videos, for just about any piece of software you would ever use, with help available for beginners and experts alike. Access to the entire library is by subscription (around $25 per month at the time this was being written), and it's some of the best money I've ever spent; everything I now know how to do—building websites, designing books, laying out covers, editing audio and video—I've learned at these sites.

Hardware is mostly a question of something much simpler. Read the manual. Especially if what you've bought is expensive. Having a video camera with high definition video and audio is no good to you if it's a mode you actually need to *turn on*, but *never did*. I figure that for every $50 you're spending over $500, it's worth reading the manual one more time. Over $1000, and you should be able to pass a quiz on the contents.

The **Static Studio** is *daunted* by how complicated technology seems to master.
The **Dynamic Studio** works proactively to attain that mastery.

How the rest of this chapter works

Rather than list a series of technology items as headings, I've listed teaching *solutions*, and then indicated which items you would need if you want to make these ideas a reality.

That way, your focus can be on the solutions themselves, rather than the toys, which really are just a means to an end.

The aim is not for you to leave with a thorough understanding as to exactly *how* to do each of these things (that would take a book in its own right...I'm working on it...), but for you to leave the chapter excited that such things are even options in the first place, and hungry to start getting the technology that makes it possible.

Annual Studio CD

Featuring a track from every student in the studio, this ends up being a much-anticipated item at the end-of-year recital or presentation evening, and a compelling way to celebrate the very best of the year-that-was.

Get an artistic student to design the cover. Play teaser tracks to students at the end of lessons in the lead up to the release. (Particularly their *own* track)

Launch it with great fanfare at a Big Studio event, watch the students queue up to get their copies.

Then in next year's advertisements, highlight the fact that *your studio has it's own CD label(!)*, and that every student gets a chance to star. Enjoy the astonishment that follows.

What you need: A good microphone; Digital Audio Workstation Software such as Logic, Cubase or Pro Tools (for mixing, editing and mastering); Indesign (to finalise cover design and performance notes); high resolution scanner, if you're using student artwork, Print On Demand CD service such as CreateSpace.com—you can then set it up so that parents can order their own copies online.

The **Static Studio** has *studio recitals* with performances that students can *remember*. The **Dynamic Studio** creates *recordings* with performances that can be *relived any time*.

Your own YouTube Video Channel

Featuring (very) selected performances of students in your studio, this is a showcase that literally presents the best of your studio to the whole world. You'd obviously need the family's permission before posting video like this online, but the Channel itself would be a readily accessible and growing testament to the results your studio produces, while the videos themselves can easily be embedded if your studio has a website—or for that matter, embedded in your students' own websites or Facebook pages.

You can also then highlight the channel in any advertising for your studio—instead of simply *claiming* that your studio produces excellent results, you'll be able to *demonstrate* it.

But perhaps the biggest impact the Channel will have is as a *meaningful reward* for deserving students. With you being picky about what makes the cut, and the Channel being viewable by anybody on the planet, having a performance listed on your YouTube channel is an accolade any student will be proud of: you're not just telling them "well done", you're telling them that they're *worthy of being an example.*

What you need: A YouTube account; a good quality video camera, ideally with a good quality microphone as a separate input; permission from the student's parents.

The **Static Studio** is YouTube *savvy*, and *recommends videos* they've found to students. The **Dynamic Studio** is a YouTube *contributor*, and *creates videos* that end up being recommended by others.

Instant replays

Sports coaches have been using this technique for years, as they try to help athletes see for themselves just what it is that they're doing when they play—a third-person perspective on their own technique that is *only* possible if the coach is able to both *record* and *replay* passages of play.

The idea works in a similar way in music teaching studios. Instead of the student playing and then you giving your comments, you can record your student playing, and then you can *both* sit back, listen, and come up with recommendations together. It allows for "same side of the desk" teaching, and helps the student to hear (and see) issues they might miss when they're otherwise too caught up in actually *playing* the piece.

What you need: A good quality video camera cabled to a monitor so the student can see the playbacks straight away.

 In the **Static Studio** the student plays, and then *turns to the teacher* for feedback. In the **Dynamic Studio** the student is able to listen to what they just played, and then *works with the teacher* to create feedback.

Studio Stationery Factory

Every initiative you dream up for your studio is going to need support material to *announce* it, *promote* it, *manage* it, and then ultimately *wrap it up*. The result is a constant need for printed resources: brochures, flyers, certificates, practice competition sheets, performance feedback surveys, parent information records, posters, programs, leaderboards...

Most teachers are faced with two choices at this point, both bad. They can either design the support material themselves using something clunky like Microsoft Word, and make their Big New Idea look like a 4th grader's geography project. Or they can use generic pre-designed resources that are almost—but not quite—what they're after.

Having the skills and software to be your own graphic designer gives you a third option, and represents *power*: you'll be able to launch many, many more ideas, with greater impact, and at a fraction of the cost.

What you need: Adobe Indesign, and the skills to use it well. A Lynda.com subscription for the software training; *Before and After Magazine* for the graphic design skills you'd need to make it look good. You'll make back every cent you spend.

The **Static Studio** *has stocks* of generic certificates, stickers and Microsoft Word Templates, and then tries to *find* the resource that's *closest* to what they need. The **Dynamic Studio** *designs* their own resources, so that they can *create exactly* what they need.

Studio Magazine

Once you become handy with a professional design program like Indesign, an otherwise daunting project like a studio magazine is really not as difficult as it sounds.

As any magazine editor will tell you, one of the secrets is lots—and I mean *lots*—of great photographs. Students love to see pictures of themselves, especially if the accompanying information has something nice to say about them.

As to the content otherwise, it's completely up to you: recaps of the year-that-was, student profiles, where-are-they-now style interviews with former students who have gone on to bigger things, articles, quizzes, composer trivia, practice hints, competition announcements...it's your magazine. Go nuts, your students will *love* it.

What you need: Indesign, and the skills to use it well. A Lynda.com subscription for the software training; *Before and After Magazine* for the graphic design skills you'd need to make it look good. Don't forget also a printing budget—a full colour magazine can be expensive, even when printed digitally—but , well designed, it's worth every cent for the impact it can have.

Check out www.magcloud.com for some examples of music-studio sized enterprises who have produced magazines of their own.

The **Static Studio** *has* interesting magazines available for parents to *browse* while they're waiting. The **Dynamic Studio** *creates* interesting magazines, for parents to *take home* (and show to *other* parents)

Aural and Theory Training Games Machine

We've looked elsewhere in this book at the difficulty of trying to find time for aural and theory training within the lesson itself. One way to relieve some of the pressure is to make use of dead time pre-and-post lessons—the idea is that rather than students just *waiting*, they could be using the time to complete aural and theory drills on your studio computer.

Obviously it's no substitute for the sort of one-on-one explanations and troubleshooting you can give in a lesson proper, but it's a perfectly valid way for them to drill concepts they already understand. In fact, if drilling is the aim, it's a much more efficient way to work through lots of examples than manually creating each question during a lesson—most computer-based training produces *randomly generated* questions, and is *self-marking;* unlike a mere textbook, this is a drill partner that never runs out of activities to complete.

There are several online resources that provide free training, including insidemusicteaching.com, but if you want to track your student's results then it's worth purchasing a commercially available package—too many options to list here.

What you need: Aural and/or theory training software, or internet access to use the online versions. Headphones so students don't drive you nuts while they're doing their training.

 The **Static Studio** handles theory with *pen and paper*, so students can complete the *limited set* of *given drills* in their textbook, and then *hand-marks* every question. The **Dynamic Studio** uses *software-based training* which *randomly* generates *limitless* questions, which are *automatically marked* as it goes.

Repertoire Browser

We looked more closely at this earlier in the book (➡ 168-170), but in essence, a Repertoire Browser is a centralised and accessible collection of recordings, sorted by level so that the student can *preview* and *choose* the pieces that are coming up for them.

So where do these recordings come from? You can make them *yourself*. Or you can *use recordings of your students* playing these pieces; sampled from previous recitals, or recorded especially for your Repertoire Browser project. Or you can *source the recordings online*—you can normally find performances of just about anything you'd need on YouTube. Whatever method you use, the easiest way to make them accessible is to assemble them into a YouTube playlist, and give your students the URL.

If you can add your own marketing-copy-style description of each piece, and stills of the score that the student can follow while they listen, then so much the better.

There's an example of how this works in the Repertoire Browser at www.insidemusicteaching.com.

What you need: Unless you're planning on pointing them to existing recordings, you'll need a microphone, digital-audio-workstation software, and the skills to use them both. Otherwise, you'll need the time to track these recordings down, and then assemble and catalogue them into a playlist.

The **Static Studio** *assigns pieces* to students.
The **Dynamic Studio** lets students
window-shop for their new repertoire.

Virtual Concerto Performances

Many studios will end up with students who are advanced enough to play concertos, but will never get the chance to perform it with anything more than a piano reduction of the orchestral part. You'll already know that armed with a *Music Minus One* recording (I think they're still the only company doing this?), it's always been possible to give them a taste of playing with an orchestra, but if you're also able to make your own recordings, you can go one better.

Instead of just *playing along* with the *Music Minus One* track, having your own recording software means you can actually *mix in* the student's own performance, to create a virtual concerto.

We looked earlier at the possibility of a Studio CD; how impressive would a Studio CD of *concerto performances* be? If you've got the students capable of playing the repertoire, then the technology definitely exists for you to make that a reality.

What you need: A good microphone, digital-audio-workstation software (DAW), and the know-how to use it. And the appropriate Music Minus One recording. (you can get them from http://musicminusone.com/)

 The **Static Studio** will provide an *accompanist* so that students can perform concerto mockups. The **Dynamic Studio** will help the student create a *virtual performance*, with a *full orchestral recording*.

Endlessly Replayable Demonstrations

Much of teaching is based on demonstration, but demonstrations tend to *deflate* over time; no matter how clear your explanation might have been at the lesson on Tuesday, by the time Friday rolls around, the student's recollection can be decidedly fuzzy—or actively inaccurate.

The key to solving this is to be able to capture demonstrations, which means not just to be able to record, but being able to record *instantly*, with no setting up required. With the DAW software running all the time, the microphone in position and on, all you'd have to do is push the red button on the computer screen, and then give the demonstration you were going to give anyway.

The only additional steps you need to take are to quickly save out the recording as an MP3, and then email it to your student at the end of the lesson—the disruption to the actual lesson itself really should be minimal.

They then have an available-any-time resource that allows them to relive your explanation whenever they need it...which saves you from having to teach exactly the same thing again next lesson.

What you need: A good microphone, digital-audio-workstation software (DAW), and the know-how to use it. And your recording software loaded and live before every lesson, ready for genuine one-click recording.

The **Static Studio** *demonstrates concepts* to students and hopes that it will stick. The **Dynamic Studio** *creates booster shots* that the students can take home, and administer any time they need to.

Studio TV(!)

Unthinkable just a few years ago, unless you had a six figure budget and years of training, but now with relatively inexpensive software such as *BoinxTV Home* or Telestream's *Wirecast*, it's very easy to create professional looking studio news broadcasts. As long as you film yourself or your students in front of a green screen, then the software allows you to easily add in backgrounds, lower third captions (to identify performers or speakers), and then assemble the raw footage into a tightly-cut news piece.

The result is a TV-style broadcast that gives you a whole new vehicle for highlighting news and achievements in your studio—all done with your studio computer, your video camera, a green backdrop, some reasonable lighting, and software that cost a few hundred dollars. Post the results to your website, or create your own YouTube studio news channel.

The possibilities this opens up are endless—particularly if you allow students to be reporters—and students will be hugely excited to feature in each instalment.

What you need: Software such as Telestream's Wirecast (Mac or PC), or BoinxTV (Mac only), or Adobe Presenter (PC only) plus the computer, video camera and green screen.

Oh, and students who want to be on TV. (That's usually no problem)

 The **Static Studio** puts out the occasional *newsletter* done in Microsoft Word. The **Dynamic Studio** has their own *broadcast channel*, with TV-style news updates.

Remote lessons

Perfect for students who are temporarily living overseas, students who live too far out of town for travel to be convenient, or even for additional help midweek for students with major performances coming up. As long as there is a computer at both ends with a camera inbuilt or attached, broadband internet, and both computers are running software such as Skype or Facetime, then there's no reason that remote lessons couldn't be conducted whenever you needed them—even if the student is not in the same hemisphere.

A massively underused opportunity, but which will grow as broadband speeds continue to get faster, allowing for ever more high definition video and sound.

What you need: Broadband internet for both teacher and student, video conferencing software like Skype or Facetime, attached or inbuilt cameras, and, ideally, high quality microphone and speakers at both ends.

The **Static Studio** runs excellent lessons in their *own studio*.
The **Dynamic Studio** can run excellent lessons *anywhere in the world*.

Your own method books

If you've ever been frustrated by the content of the method books you use, or the order in which things are presented, or what you feel might be glaring omissions, and have any sort of skills as a composer, then you might want to consider developing your *own* method book.

Using a print-on-demand service like MagCloud or CreateSpace, there's almost no cost in producing the book in the first place—the only cost would be to the students as they order their own copy.

As any university student will tell you, there's nothing quite like being able to study with the professor who wrote the text; the fact that you've produced your own method will speak volumes about both your creativity, and the depth with which you think about educating your students.

What you need: Notation software such as Sibelius or Finale. Design and layout software like Adobe Indesign, and the skills to use it. An account with a Print on Demand service such as CreateSpace, Lightning Source or MagCloud.

The **Static Studio** thinks very carefully about the *choice* of method books for their studio. The **Dynamic Studio** thinks very carefully about *what to put* in their *own* method book.

Sister Studios in Far Away Places

Video conferencing software like Skype or Facetime doesn't just make it possible to work with your own students in their own homes; your entire studio could start collaborating with other studios anywhere in the world.

So instead of workshops being limited to whoever will fit in your studio, it can also include whoever is able to watch the live stream. Students who play at your end will be able to get feedback from students at their end, together with input from whoever teaches those students. And vice-versa.

It's one thing to be told by your teacher that your dynamics are exciting. It's another entirely to hear that from a fellow student in another hemisphere.

What you need: Same requirements as for remote teaching: broadband internet for both your studio and theirs, video conferencing software like Skype or Facetime, attached or inbuilt cameras, and, ideally, high quality microphone and speakers at both ends. And a reliable international clock so you can synchronise times.

The **Static Studio** will *occasionally* have their students work with other teachers *in town*. The **Dynamic Studio** will *frequently* have their students work with other teachers *from all over the world*.

...the tip of the technological iceberg

The list of *actual* possibilities dwarfs what has been so briefly listed in this chapter—aside from the constant stream of emerging technologies, there are still countless teaching uses yet to be dreamed up for *existing* technology. Armed with nothing but a decades old 4-track mixer and a $50 microphone, a creative teacher can engineer dozens of unique lessons.

As has been the case throughout the book, the point of the included examples was not to give a comprehensive tour, but to get your own head ticking over—necessity will be the mother of all these studio inventions, so it all starts by thinking of teaching options you *wish* were available to your studio, but currently *aren't*:

Do you, for example, want to have an **information hub** that parents can't miss, with breaking news, student-of-the-week, upcoming concert dates? Maybe it's worth installing a monitor that's visible from the parent's waiting area, plugged into a powerpoint presentation that loops through information. Updating it would take just a few minutes each week.

It's *your* studio.

You get to decide what happens.

Or perhaps you might need a way to **keep young siblings quiet** when they sit in on lessons? Is it worth having some portable gaming options and headphones? Or a television that loops Pixar movies?

It's *your* studio.

You get to decide what happens.

Or maybe you want to **go bookless** for your repertoire? Is it time to explore ways that students can load all their pieces onto a tablet device, or download and print out their music as they need it? If they're working with an electronic copy, is it possible for you to make marks and comments on this electronic score?

It's *your* studio.

You get to decide what happens.

Or do you want to be better prepared for your **fortnightly improvisation lessons,** by building your own pre-recorded library of backing tracks and chord progressions for students to improvise over...and then download to work with at home?

It's *your* studio.

You get to decide what happens.

Or do you want to set up a **student-feedback system,** so that students can post recordings of their performance online, and then have other students in the studio post constructive criticism underneath?

Or do you want to have a series of **coffee-table quality photo books** capturing the best of studio events from years' past?

Or your own series of **podcasts,** with *practice advice,* or *theory lessons,* or *composer trivia,* or *student interviews...*

...this book started with a warning: that the world of your music students moves fast. That it's technology filled, exciting, rapidly changing and bursting with possibility.

But here's the thing: *it's actually the very same world you're in too.* You don't have to have your nose pressed up against the glass, wishing that you were part of it: you're standing in it, right now. For any teacher of a Dynamic Studio, that's a giddyingly exciting prospect.

The **Static Studio** *uses* technology to keep up with what other studios offer. The **Dynamic Studio** *mines* technology for teaching options that no other teaching studio has even thought of yet.

What's next:

There's one more studio upgrade that we haven't talked about yet. It's actually the only upgrade that a Dynamic Studio is impossible without; left till last, so that if you only remember one thing from this book, you remember this.

The Ultimate Upgrade
You, version 2.0

The Ultimate Upgrade

ONE MORE THING, BEFORE WE GO our separate ways, and I leave you to make whatever you will of the invitation that is *The Dynamic Studio.*

Given that this book may have been written long ago by the time you're actually reading it, a certain way for me to look like an idiot is to hold something up as being "the *ultimate* upgrade". With new teaching resources and technologies launching all the time, something is bound to come along that will trump whatever I choose to champion.

But I promise you, nothing will. I am absolutely certain of the call I'm about to make:

Of all the teaching tools that you depend on, nothing is quite so fundamental and worth upgrading—and nothing ever will be—as, well, *you.*

This is because your studio *is* you.

It will thrive or wither, astonish or fail to engage, excel or hack in the weeds according to your efforts, creativity, empathy and persistence. It's a product of your *imagination*, and—above all else—is entirely dependent on your *skills.*

This book has been reluctant to impose ceilings, but there is one that's very real, and entirely unbreachable:

...your studio will not be greater than the skills available to power it.

Your skills. And not just the musical ones.

All too often though, the diplomas on the studio walls represent the last sustained and serious upskilling that a music teacher will ever do, the seals and signatures conferring not just a degree, but closure: Your training is *done.* Finished. Behind you. Congratulations.

It's very easy for the year immediately after graduation to pass with no further upgrades. And the year after that. And the next...and so on, until suddenly its been 20 years since this dog really learned new tricks.

Don't say it can't happen to you. That's *exactly* what happens in tens of thousands of music studios around the world. The teacher develops expert musical skills early in their career, but beyond attending the occasional conferences or workshop, never seriously develops beyond where they first arrived. They've been busy, they've been conscientious and organised and energetic and all those good things, but otherwise essentially unchanged, undeveloped.

> **...your studio will not be greater than the skills available to power it."**

Static.

None of this would matter, except that a music studio is not ultimately limited by what the teacher can *imagine*—that's the easy part—but what they have the *ability to deliver*. This is a hugely important distinction: an idea without the means to enact it is merely a pipedream.

When *opportunities* and *solutions* are strangled by *doubt*

It's not just ambitious initiatives that are hamstrung by skill deficiencies. Solutions to thoroughly everyday teaching problems can be stillborn if the teacher even so much as *wonders* if they really have the requisite skillset to implement them. This doubt manifests as hesitations, as should-I-really-do-this; little voices that urge caution, overseeing the extinguishment of countless ideas, great and small.

We've all experienced this doubt at times. It's a horrible feeling, because we know deep down that the solution we will end up adopting is informed not by excellence or best practice, but by *prudence* and *compromise* and *I'm-not-so-sure-I'm-up-to-this*.

For the Dynamic Studio, it represents a dramatic thinning of options, to a point where it can become easier just to leave things as they are. When your skills are not constantly moving forward, eventually the Status Quo is all you'll have left open to you.

So, for example, in the wake of a recital that had poor student-accompanist co-ordination, a teacher's Dynamic Studio instincts might be to increase the amount of time students get to rehearse directly with the accompaniment part next time.

This is a great *idea*. It makes *perfect sense*. But like any other idea, it's entirely contingent upon specific skills to see it through: in this case, unless the teacher is going to pay to have an accompanist on standby in every lesson, *that teacher needs to be able to play the piano well enough to accompany their own students.*

> "When your skills are not constantly moving forward, eventually the Status Quo is all you'll have left open to you."

If they *do* have that skill, then a whole new lesson solution has just opened up for them. If they don't (and a lot of instrumental teachers don't) then it's checkmate, and the idea remains as an idea. It may well have been a smart solution to a tricky problem, but that means nothing if there's no way of getting it done.

This is not a failure of imagination. This is constraint by skillset. It happens every day, in every studio, vetoing our best laid plains.

Consider another studio, wrestling this time not with a *problem*, but an *opportunity*. Let's imagine that there's a new animated movie that the teacher knows most of their students have seen, and that it has a compelling and unforgettable soundtrack. Let's also imagine that the rhythms involved happen to be brain-freezingly complex when notated.

> "...all too often, the diplomas on the studio walls represent the last sustained and serious upskilling that a music teacher will ever do..."

It would make perfect sense to seize the moment and assign students some of the pieces that appear in this soundtrack, but whether the associated rhythmic complexity ends up being merely a *challenge*, or a potential *dealbreaker* will come down to the teacher's own skills: just how strong is their own rhythm reading? Would they truly back themself to nail each of the passages they'd have to troubleshoot, first time, every time? Or will they decide having to *decode* and *explain* these rhythms is going to be more trouble than it's worth...and reluctantly (but prudently) let the opportunity slide?

Again, the limitation here is not the teacher's ability to *come up with* the concept, but their capacity to *deliver*.

There are very few ideas in this book—or outside this book—that aren't subject to such skill checks:

- Teachers whose own playing skills have been maintained so that they **can play anything their students can** will be able to give solid demonstrations of whatever their students are currently studying, together with tempting live previews of upcoming repertoire. Those who can't will have to depend on *recordings*, and *descriptions*.

- Teachers with **strong public speaking skills** will be able to compellingly introduce studio recitals, and run parent information sessions and workshops. Those who don't will either miss such opportunities to impress, or will leave parents underwhelmed when they do take the microphone.

- Teachers who are **comfortable with social networking technologies** will be able to use them in creative ways to turn their studio into a community. Those who aren't will be forced to find another way, or run a studio that networks like it's still 1980.

- Teachers who **make a point of listening to** and **reading about** the same popular music artists and bands that their students do will end up being able to make popular repertoire recommendations that feel authentic and well-informed. Those who don't will be guessing.

- Teachers with **credentials in early childhood education** will have added credibility when they advertise their music program for preschoolers, and then have professionally informed insights into the development of those young students; those who don't will have to wing it.

- Teachers who are **well versed in life-coaching, sports psychology or NLP** will be able to prepare students mentally for big competitions and auditions based on the collective expertise of the world's leading motivation and performance experts. Those who don't can only offer their own advice based on instinct, and whatever they can remember former teachers telling them.

- Teachers with a **genuine command of multiple musical styles** will be able to accommodate a wide range of student interests and tastes. Those who don't will have to fake it as best they can, or limit their studio to what they are comfortable with.

- Teachers with an understanding of **Alexander** or **Mitzvah Technique** will be able to give expert and injury-preventing posture assistance to students. Those who don't can only go on what they've been told by whoever taught them.

- Teachers with **composition skills** who are comfortable arranging works will be able to invent ensemble parts, and simplify, tailor, extend and rework solo repertoire from something that's *almost right* for a student to something that's *perfect*. Teachers without these skills are limited to off-the-rack pieces.

- Teachers who has **played in hundreds of paying gigs in a string quartet** will be well placed to run a studio that doubles as a chamber-music-for-weddings business. A teacher who has never done such work probably wouldn't think to set up such an opportunity for their students.

- Teachers with **an encyclopedic knowledge of teaching repertoire** will be able to find exciting, engaging pieces that are well-matched to the student in front of them. Teachers who don't are more likely to keep teaching the same pieces year after year.

Note that the skills don't have to be even remotely musical to still make a positive difference:

- Teachers who have skills in something even as seemingly irrelevant as **origami** or **basic stage-magic** can instantly engage—and delight—young students who otherwise are reluctant to let go of dad's leg in that first lesson. Teachers who don't will have to find some other way.

- Teachers with expertise in **amateur astronomy** can run studio workshops that are 90 minutes of playing, and then an hour of starwatching. Teachers who don't will probably end up with workshops that look like everyone else's.

- Teachers who have done a course in **radio production and presentation** could host their own segment on a community radio station—or set up their own web-based show—which can then be used to give students performance opportunities. Teachers without such skills could only listen in to such broadcasts.

- Teachers with **strong photography skills** can produce stunning records of studio recitals and individual students, and transform the studio space with a growing gallery that chronicles the studio's history. Teachers who don't will need to find a parent to take photos, or make do with whatever they can snap on their digital camera.

- Teachers who are **comfortable with using Dreamweaver or CMS/blogging platforms like WordPress** can run their own studio website. Teachers who aren't will need to pay someone to do it for them...or not be online at all.

- Teachers who are **keen joggers** can train with and then enter a studio team in the annual city Fun Run. Teachers who are not will need to find an alternative team-building exercise. (There's no shortage of alternatives, but this is an example of how a *passion* on your part can become an *asset* to the studio)

- Teachers with **design and layout training** can produce professional studio resources, from certificates to posters, program notes to theory sheets. Teachers without will have to settle for whatever bland, unprofessional results they can manage in Microsoft Word.

- Teachers with **video editing skills** are able to assemble compelling and well-edited annual studio video reviews, and individual studio portfolios that students will be showing their grandparents today, and their grand*children* in years to come. Teachers who don't aren't likely to attempt anything so ambitious.

- Teachers with **cartooning ability** will be able to create unique and engaging feedback for their students—not just reminding their students that this passage needs to be quieter, but drawing a picture of a mouse in slippers, tiptoeing. Those who are the drawing equivalent of tone-deaf (like me) will have to get by with mere words.

...a list like this could easily—*easily*—run for dozens of pages.

The point is not to feel dismayed by all the skills you don't currently have, but to be aware of the skills you do have, and understand that developing *any one of these additional skills* will unlock a fractalling branch of new studio possibilities.

So take a moment just to note what unique *abilities*, or *interests* or *passions* you might have, particularly if they're traits that your students aren't even currently aware of. How could they actively become assets for your teaching studio? And then, returning to the question that started this book...

Given the extraordinary changes music teaching finds itself surrounded by, if you had the opportunity to hit "reset" on how your studio currently operates and build it again from scratch, what might your new job look like?

...what skills are you currently lacking that are stopping you from answering that in the way you'd really love to? Are these skills something you can teach yourself? Read up on? Enrol in a course for? Watch tutorial videos online? Or even just dive into and...in the best sense of the word (and dare I say it out loud)... start *practicing?*

Remember, you're in charge in your studio—you don't have to run your proposed changes past a committee, or await permission from the executive: you *are* the executive. If the only thing holding you back is a missing skill, then seriously...

...what are you waiting for?

Enrol in that course. Search YouTube for those videos. Read that instruction manual. Buy those how-to books from Amazon. Take an expert out for lunch. Get the software package, or the microphone, or the video camera, or the calligraphy set, or whatever, and just start *working* with it...

...that's enough, right there.
The **Static Studio** reads books.
The **Dynamic Studio** makes changes.
Go: start something *astonishing.*

Philip Johnston online

www.**insidemusicteaching**.com

Free online magazine and downloadable resources.

www.**thedynamicstudio**.com

Got ideas? Join the conversation.

For **Teachers...**

The Practice Revolution
Getting Great Results from the 6 days between lessons

"This book is perhaps in the top 1% of all the things I have ever recommended. Every sentence is new and important and this goes on for 321 pages...buy the book!"
Canadian Music Educator Association Journal

I have read, ear marked, highlighted, and practically worn out this book! It is by far the best thing I've ever read on teaching music.
Customer Review on Amazon.com

For **Students...**

Practiceopedia
The Big Book of Practice Help

...there are so many good ideas here, I can't begin to list them."
European Piano Teacher's Association Magazine

"...belongs on the music stand and piano rack of every practicing musician."
American Music Teacher **Magazine**

"The ultimate reference for students...this is a 'must have' book. "
Music Teacher International

"...attention-grabbing book that gives the word "practice" a whole new meaning."
Journal of Australian Strings Association

Made in the USA
Columbia, SC
14 April 2021